"Takin' the bull by its cooked horns . . ."

—Judge Samuel B. Kent

from the factual summary, in the United States District Court
for the Southern District of Texas, Galveston, Texas
Civil Action No. G-01-491

Texas Under Six Flags

Quotes from Judge Samuel B. Kent are excerpts from his opinions, and are not a suggestion that he has reviewed or endorsed this book.

All advice and commentary herein are the opinions of the compiler and are not intended as legal advice.

Stewing in Texas

The Case of the Rustled Cookbook

Compiled by Joan Liffring-Zug Bourret
Recipes and essays by Carol Blakely

Penfield Press

Dedication & Acknowledgments

Dedicated to all compilers of recipe books and their defense lawyers

Acknowledgments: In addition to those mentioned in the text, we thank Iowans Dan Cilek and Jeremy Richardson of Iowa City, Ruth Nash of Dubuque, and many others.

Historic postcards and sayings are from the collection of Carol Blakely. They include those from the Lake County (Illinois) Discovery Museum/Curt Teich Postcard Archives and the Baxter Lane Printing Company of Amarillo, Texas from their Laff-O-Gram cards, which poke fun at Texas and Texans. The majority of Texas postcards used in this book date from the early 1900s.

Associate editors: Dwayne Bourret, Melinda Bradnan, Miriam Canter, Dorothy Crum, Esther Feske, Lindsay Keast, Maureen Patterson, Jeanne Wright, and David Wright.

Drawings by Diane Heusinkveld

Graphic designers: Julio Ramiriz, Aaron Cruse, Kathleen Timmerman, and Molly Cook, M.A.Cook Design

2200. Cow Boy thrown from a Wild Bucking Broncho.

Library of Congress Control Number 2005910822
ISBN 1572161132   ©2006 Penfield Press

CONTENTS

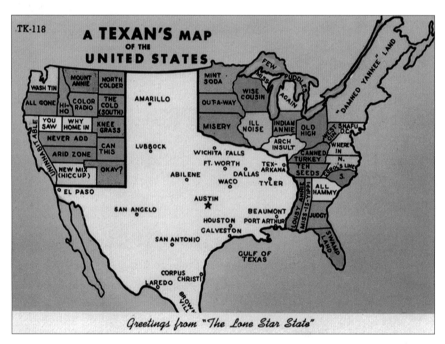

Note that Iowa, home of Penfield Press in the lawsuit, is listed as "Out-A-Way," just south of "Mint Soda" in this historic postcard by Curt Teich.

LASSOED WITHOUT WARNING!

Often in copyright cases, the participants settle problems without resorting to the courts. Notice is given to the party who may have used copyrighted text by mistake, and the problem is settled gracefully. Jim Head and Penfield Press were served by mail, without advance notice, by lawyers for *Cowboy Chow,* published in 1988, and by Cookbook Resources, L.L.C. alleging copyright infringement involving eighteen recipes used in the Penfield Press title *License to Cook Texas Style.* Dianna Stevens, who grew up in Texas, compiled the recipes with permission to use them from Jim Head of *Texas OnLine,* her source for the eighteen recipes.

Notice of the suit came in August 2001, five years after Penfield's publication of *License to Cook Texas Style.* **There is no source for easy reference to check if a recipe may be copyrighted as part of a larger editorial work. Usually recipes that are primarily ingredients and methods with minimal serving instructions are cited as copyright-free. People collecting recipes and sharing them in church and community cookbooks could face similar suits if a batch of recipes compiled in a publication accidentally duplicates similar ones in a copyrighted book. Jim Head thought the recipes on his website were copyright-free for all to use. References about copyrights cite such recipes as public domain, free for all to use even if within a book that may have original editorial text that is copyrighted.**

The aim of the copyright laws is to put intentional violators of copyright ownership out of business.

Incorporation for us offered little or no protection for our personal assets. Virtually all assets of a small publishing corporation as well as the assets of its individual officers may be confiscated to pay fines and legal fees. For Joan Liffring-Zug Bourret, age 72, president of Penfield Press, all her retirement savings and most property were at risk in this suit. Exempt in Iowa, according to research by Attorney Anne Loomis, are $2,000 worth of clothing, one shotgun, and either one rifle or musket. **If a jury decides that the defendant is innocent, a federal judge still has the power to overturn the jury decision and fine the defendant.**

There are dozens, if not hundreds, of recipes published in books, newspaper food features, magazines, and still available on the Internet, similar to or duplicating those cited in this lawsuit against Penfield Press. It is virtually impossible to know if recipes are in an out-of-print book or have comments claimed to be original and copyright-protected. In this case, the phrase "great with meats," the English translation of Pico de Gallo, beak of the rooster, and serving instructions for eating a common Texas snack out of a bag were cited as original expressions in the court document denying dismissal of the case. Unless judges, attorneys, and case researchers are familiar with recipes and the commonality of language used in many recipes, it is difficult for them to determine original language warranting copyright protection. This book recounts what happened to a small publisher in 2001.

— The Editor

"If face powder catches a man, then baking powder keeps him."
—Carol Blakely

She's no shy goose,
Jump on your cayuse, —

THE LAWSUIT BEGINS

Theatre For The Case
The United States District Court
for the Southern District of Texas, Galveston Division
Federal Judge Samuel B. Kent
The Galveston, Texas, Federal Courthouse
Civil Action No. G-01-491*

Jury trial date: August 2002
Estimated fines, court costs, and legal fees
for the defendants if Penfield Press loses:
$400,000 ($20,000 per recipe!)

Cost of appeal to the next court:
Budget a 10-percent bond and $75,000!

*All documents in this case are available in the Galveston Federal Courthouse.

JUDGE SAMUEL B. KENT
and
THE "ROCKET DOCKET"

The Honorable Judge Samuel B. Kent was scheduled to try the copyright case of Judy Barbour's *Cowboy Chow* and Cookbook Resources, L.L.C. v. *License to Cook Texas Style* by Penfield Press in August 2002. **"Rocket Docket" refers to courts who move cases from filing to trial in an abbreviated time (or in substantially less time than most courts).** A Galveston lawyer, Judge Kent graduated from the University of Texas School of Law in 1975. After fifteen years in private practice in Galveston, in 1990 he was appointed a federal judge for life by President George Bush.

He has many admirers for his wit in footnotes and writings. Attorneys often exchange selective portions of his writings, including this especially colorful example:

THE JACK RABBIT AIRPORT OPINION

"Defendant will again be pleased to know that regular limousine service is available from Hobby Airport, even to the steps of this humble courthouse, which has got lights, indoor plummin', 'lectric doors, and all sorts of new stuff, almost like them big courthouses back East."

—Judge Samuel B. Kent

Excerpts from this famous case follow:

STEPHANIE SMITH v. COLONIAL PENN INSURANCE COMPANY
Civil Action No. G-96-503. United States District Court,
S.D. Texas, Galveston Division. Nov. 6, 1996

ORDER DENYING MOTION TO TRANSFER . . .

"This is a breach of contract case based on an insurance contract entered into by Plaintiff and Defendant. Now before the Court is Defendant's October 11, 1996 Motion to Transfer Venue from the Galveston Division to the Houston Division of the United States District Court for the Southern District of Texas pursuant to 28 U.S.C.=A7 1404(a). For the reasons set forth below, the Motion is DENIED.

"Defendant's request for a transfer of venue is centered around the fact that Galveston does not have a commercial airport into which Defendant's employees and corporate representatives may fly and out of which they may be expediently whisked to the federal courthouse in Galveston. Rather, Defendant contends that it will be faced with the huge 'inconvenience' of flying into Houston and driving less than forty miles to the Galveston courthouse, an act that will 'encumber' it with 'unnecessary driving time and expenses.' The Court certainly does not wish to encumber any litigant with such an onerous burden. The Court, being somewhat familiar with the Northeast, notes that perceptions about travel are different in that part of the country than they are in Texas. A litigant in that part of the country could cross several states in a few hours and might be shocked at having to travel fifty miles to try a case, but in this vast state of Texas, such a travel distance would not be viewed with any surprise or consternation. . . . Defendant should be assured that it is not embarking on a three-week-long trip via covered wagons when it travels to Galveston.

"Rather, Defendant will be pleased to discover that the highway is paved and lighted all the way to Galveston, and thanks to the efforts of this Court's predecessor, Judge Roy Bean,* the trip should be free of rustlers, hooligans, or vicious varmints of unsavory kind.

*In a footnote, Judge Samuel B. Kent quotes the message on this card.

"Moreover, the speed limit was recently increased to seventy miles per hour on most of the road leading to Galveston, so Defendant should be able to hurtle to justice at lightning speed.

". . . To assuage Defendant's worries about the inconvenience of the drive, the Court notes that Houston's Hobby Airport is located about equal drive time from downtown Houston and the Galveston courthouse. Defendant will likely find it an easy, traffic-free ride to Galveston as compared to a congested, construction-riddled drive to downtown Houston. The Court notes that any inconvenience suffered in having to drive to Galveston may likely be offset by the peacefulness of the ride and the scenic beauty of the sunny isle.

"The convenience of the witnesses and the parties is generally a primary concern of this Court when considering transfer motions. However, vague statements about the convenience of unknown and unnamed witnesses is

EDITOR'S NOTE: *Judge Roy Bean was a Justice of the Peace for about twenty years on the Rio Grande in the Big Bend area of South Texas. Once, an unidentified man was found dead, wearing a pistol with forty dollars in his pocket; the judge confiscated the pistol and fined the man forty dollars for carrying a concealed weapon. (Judge Bean is a distant relative of Penfield editor Melinda Bradnan.)*

insufficient to convince this Court that the convenience of the witnesses and the parties would be best served by transferring venue. . . .

"In the Court's view, even if all the witnesses, documents, and evidence relevant to this case were located within walking distance of the Houston Division Courthouse, the inconvenience caused by retaining the case in this Court would be minimal at best in this age of convenient travel, communication, discovery, and trial testimony preservation. The Galveston Division Courthouse* is only about fifty miles from the Houston Division Courthouse. **It is not as if the key witnesses will be asked to travel to the wilds of Alaska or the furthest reaches on the Continental United States.**"

In a footnote Judge Kent states, "**. . . it is not this Court's concern how Plaintiff gets here, whether it be by plane, train, automobile, horseback, foot, or on the back of a huge Texas jack rabbit, as long as Plaintiff is here at the proper date and time.**"

© *Baxter Lane Printing Company*

(See page 124 for more information about the Galveston Courthouse.)

COOKS IN THE STEW

Plaintiffs

Judy Barbour* of Bay City, Texas, has published several cookbooks in addition to *Cowboy Chow*. Wife of a Texan with a hunting business in Jackson, Wyoming, she authored *Elegant Elk, Delicious Deer,* according to biographical information printed in *Cowboy Chow*. Ms. Barbour indicated that Cookbook Resources, L.L.C. had an interest in a new edition of *Cowboy Chow* and that the sale of *License to Cook Texas Style* had damaged her reputation.

Cookbook Resources, L.L.C. is owned by Sheryn R. Jones of Highland Village, Texas. She had a distinguished career as a cookbook consultant and served as a vice president of a publishing company. An award winner, she currently publishes and distributes many cookbooks.

*Others with the name Judy Barbour: Not all persons with this name publish cookbooks. Judy Barbour, librarian, in North Carolina, cares for two horses, three dogs, and assorted fish in goldfish ponds. This Judy says she does not cook.

Plaintiff Riders

G.P. Hardy, III, an old friend of Judy Barbour, plaintiff, practices law in Houston and Bay City, Texas. He is a noted litigator, winning million-dollar settlements.

John Timothy Byrd, a Yale University graduate, attended the University of Texas School of Law. He assisted G. P. Hardy in this recipe lawsuit.

Defendants

James Head, Rockwall, Texas, stated that he is the owner of an Internet website called *Texas OnLine* and that he is a gourmet chef with more than five hundred cookbooks. He said, "I previously owned the Yahoo Cake Company and have also developed recipes of my own." He stated that Dianna Stevens asked permission to include the recipes in her cookbook and, "I granted her permission, provided she credit me and the website . . . in my belief, she had full right to use them in the cookbook she was preparing. . . . I consider the recipes put on my website to be public domain recipes, free for anyone to use." Mr. Head asked a friend, **Attorney Fred Klody,** to represent him.

Penfield Press is owned by **Joan Liffring-Zug Bourret,** Iowa City, Iowa. "Have you ever been in Texas?" a Texas attorney asked the Penfield Press publisher. For more than forty-five years, this photographer and writer has photographed and produced images and books about Texans and Texas. Joan's photographs taken in 1959 at Shallowater, Texas, near Lubbock, resulted in a book titled *Jim and Alan on a Cotton Farm,* which was used in public schools nationwide as part of a series about the life and work of an American farm family.

In 1979 Joan and her late husband, John D. Zug, launched Penfield Press with the publication of *The American Gothic Cookbook* featuring recipes from American artist Grant Wood and his family and friends. This was followed by books about Czechs, including *Czechoslovak Culture: Recipes and Traditions,* featuring Joan's color photographs of Czech folk dancers from West Texas and the Czechs in Corpus Christi.

The book *German-American Life* included Joan's photographs taken in the Texas towns of New Braunfels, Fredericksburg, and Galveston. Penfield Press has released more than one hundred books including others featuring recipes, proverbs, and folk arts.

In 1996 Joan was elected to the Iowa Women's Hall of Fame. Her photographs are in many collections, including The Metropolitan Museum of Art in New York City. The Iowa State Historical Society has archived more than 500,000 negatives of Joan's work.

Defense Riders

Attorneys:

John M. Bickel, attorney, Shuttleworth & Ingersoll, Cedar Rapids, Iowa, advised Defendant Joan Liffring-Zug Bourret to retain a Texas attorney. **Michael O. McDermott** of this firm also consulted.

Ruth Teleki of Houston, first cousin of the late Penfield Press co-founder, John Zug, suggested calling the law firm of Baker Botts in Houston.

Karen Tripp, Houston attorney and copyright specialist, became attorney in charge for Penfield Press at the suggestion of Baker Botts. Attorney Tripp and Ruth Teleki contributed recipes for a trouble-free edition of *License to Cook Texas Style: Revised and Expanded.*

Tim Grady of Iowa City formed Penfield Books, a new corporation, to publish new titles.

Clint Van Zee, attorney and family friend, Van Horn, Iowa, now of Colorado, advised that there was no choice but to "develop a vigorous defense."

Dean Carrington of Iowa City assisted.

Travis C. Broesche, acceptable to both sides, agreed to serve as a mediator: but plaintiffs did not want to mediate. Penfield Press began to prepare for an August 2002 jury trial in Galveston.

Tom Riley of Cedar Rapids and Iowa City, Iowa, agreed to serve as a trial lawyer pro hoc vice with Karen Tripp. Attorney Riley, an old friend of Joan's, has a national reputation as a distinguished trial lawyer, winning dozens of high-profile cases. (See page 117 for more about Riley.)

Special Riders:

Carol Blakely of Dallas, owner of the Internet site *Jalapeño Café,* volunteered to help with the defense of Penfield Press and to serve as a recipe expert. Penfield Books published Carol's *Tales of Texas Tables.*

Physicians Craig Champion and **John Kammermeyer** asked that the trial date be changed from August to October 2002 because of Joan's allergies. The request was denied by the court.

Ed Hirs, III, of Houston, an authority on multi-million dollar corporate valuations, agreed to assist Attorney Tripp.

THE FIRST HEARING

Defense Attorney Karen Tripp considered hitching a ride on a passing Texas jack rabbit to the Galveston courthouse for the first hearing in the lawsuit against Penfield Press. A transcript of the hearing is printed here in its entirety except for attorney addresses and phone numbers.

TRANSCRIPT OF THE FIRST HEARING

IN THE UNITED STATES DISTRICT COURT
FOR THE SOUTHERN DISTRICT OF TEXAS
GALVESTON DIVISION

JUDY BARBOUR,
COOKBOOK RESOURCES, L.L.C.
V.
JAMES HEAD, PENFIELD PRESS, INC.
No. G-01-CV-491
GALVESTON, TEXAS
NOVEMBER 7, 2001
TRANSCRIPT OF RULE 16 HEARING
BEFORE THE HONORABLE SAMUEL B. KENT
APPEARANCES:
FOR PLAINTIFFS:
    TIM BYRD
    Hardy & Johns
FOR DEFENDANT PENFIELD PRESS:
    KAREN BRYANT TRIPP
    Attorney at Law

THE COURT: Be seated, please. I have a couple [sic] that we should have gotten earlier that slipped through the cracks, for which I apologize. There are two of these in sequence. The first one is G-01-491, Judy Barbour, et al. versus James Head, et al. Who's here for the plaintiffs?

MR. BYRD: Tim Bird [sic] for the plaintiff, Your Honor.

THE COURT: Hello, sir. And for the defendants?

MS. TRIPP: Karen Trip [sic] for Defendant Penfield Press, Your Honor. Defendant Heard [sic] is not represented.

THE COURT: What is this about?

MR. BYRD: Your Honor, this is a copyright infringement claim over a portion of a cookbook written by my client, Judy Barbour.

THE COURT: Somebody purloined the recipes and put them in another book?

MR. BYRD: Well, that's our allegation, Your Honor. And there is a defendant who's not yet appeared in the case, the individual, Mr. Head. We indicated in our case management plan—Mr. Head is undergoing cancer treatment and he's just recently accepted service by waiver. And I've actually agreed to try and figure out more with Miss Tripp what this case is about and proceed against them and give him some additional time for things to sort out.

THE COURT: How much is at controversy?

MR. BYRD: We think it's in six figures, Your Honor, but we need to do some discovery to insure [sic] exactly how much.

THE COURT: Where did all this take place?

MR. BYRD: Here in Texas, Your Honor, in the Southern District. Miss Barbour is a resident of Matagorda County and she's a Texas resident and wrote a Texas cookbook. And Mr. Head is in Rockwall County. And Penfield is up in Iowa, I believe. Is that right?

MS. TRIPP: Yes, Your Honor.

THE COURT: What were these recipes for?

MS. TRIPP: Pardon me, Your Honor?

THE COURT: What were these recipes for?

MR. BYRD: Your Honor, it was a—Miss Barbour wrote a book called "Cowboy Chow" that's been in print for a number of years. It was, sort of, Texas lifestyle, tidbits of history, and a bunch of southwestern cuisine that many of—which she had actually developed or they were family recipes. That—that's our contention and that's what she says.

THE COURT: Exotic stuff or, like, corn bread?

MR. BYRD: Some of it's corn bread and some of it's more exotic, Your Honor. I mean, some of it is, you know, it's stuff that would be in other cookbooks.

THE COURT: All right.

MR. BYRD: And it's only a portion of it. Let me make clear to the Court, it's not—they didn't rip the covers off of the whole book—

THE COURT: No, I understand.

MR. BYRD: —and republish it. But it's in excess of a dozen recipes we contend have been misappropriated.

THE COURT: All right. Is this jury?

MR. BYRD: Yes, Your Honor. We've requested a jury.

THE COURT: How long will it take to present the cookbook caper?

MS. TRIPP: We believe, Your Honor, that the matter will be decided under dispositive motions.

THE COURT: Well, assuming that it goes to trial, how much time will it take?

MR. BYRD: Your Honor, I think—we've spoken about it and we had a little longer period of time. I think we could probably try it by mid summer [sic]. Karen? Again. I'm not sure.

THE COURT: No. How many days do you need to try it?

MR. BYRD: Oh, I think about three days, Your Honor, three or four days.

THE COURT: That's fine. We'll try it in three days. Each side will get a day and a half. **I take it, nobody's starving to death over this controversy.**

MR. BYRD: No, Your Honor, not to my knowledge, other than Mr. Head. Candidly, I don't know his circumstances or conditions. We'll find out.

THE COURT: All right. Let's—in contemplation of his punitive participation, I'll set this trial on the jury docket for August the 26th of '02. I'm going to close discovery on August the 9th. Pretrial order will be due, please, in the jury format by August 16th. Pretrial conference, the week of August the 19th. Plaintiff shall designate experts, if any, and tender their reports by May the 17th. Defendant shall designate experts, if any, and tender their reports by July—excuse me, by June the 28th. And I'm not going to set a deadline for dispositive motions. If you think you're entitled to file them addressing a matter of law, not nuances on the evidence, let's get those on file as quickly as possible. Responses will be due in 20 days and no response will be permitted nor required. If you're going to mediate the case, I'll leave the timing of that entirely to you. Advise the Court as to your joint selection of the mediator by the 30th of December of this year. Is there anything else we need to talk about today?

MR. BYRD: No, Your Honor.

20—

MS. TRIPP: There is a dispositive motion already pending, Your Honor.

THE COURT: All right. Go ahead and respond to that.

MR. BYRD: Yes, Your Honor, we will. Our response date is next week.

THE COURT: Good. All right. Thank you both very much. It's nice to see each of you.

MR. BYRD: Thank you, Your Honor.

OFFICIAL COURT REPORTER: JEANETTE C. BYERS, RPR, CSR PROCEEDINGS RECORDED BY MECHANICAL STENOGRAPH, TRANSCRIPT PRODUCED BY COMPUTER-AIDED TRANSCRIPTION
Jeanette Byers, CSR, RPR (409) 766-3559

Defense Attorney Karen Tripp, left, and Ruth Teleki, both of Houston, are shown in front of the Galveston Post Office and Federal Courthouse. They assisted in compiling a new version of License to Cook Texas Style: Revised and Expanded, *during the course of the lawsuit. Penfield Books was founded to continue publishing most titles.*

JUDGE KENT REFUSES TO DISMISS THE LAWSUIT

Before the initial hearing, Penfield Press Attorney Karen Tripp filed a motion to have the lawsuit dismissed. With anxiety we awaited the judge's decision, which came in December 2001. Federal District Court Judge Samuel B. Kent allowed the lawsuit to proceed to a jury trial set for August 2002.

EDITOR'S NOTE: *We have bold-faced selected portions of the text and enlarged others for emphasis in Judge Samuel B. Kent's decision.*

IN THE UNITED STATES DISTRICT COURT
FOR THE SOUTHERN DISTRICT OF TEXAS
GALVESTON DIVISION

JUDY BARBOUR and
COOKBOOK RESOURCES, L.L.C.
    Plaintiffs,
V.
JAMES HEAD and
PENFIELD PRESS, INC.
    Defendants.
CIVIL ACTION NO. G-01-491

ORDER GRANTING IN PART DEFENDANT PENFIELD PRESS'S MOTION TO DISMISS

This case involves a rustled cowboy cookbook. On August 13, 2001, Plaintiffs Judy Barbour ("Barbour") and Cookbook Resources, L.L.C. ("Cookbook Resources") filed causes of action for copyright infringement, unfair competition through misappropriation, and conversion, with which **they're fixin' to brand** Defendants James Head ("Head") and Penfield Press, Inc. ("Penfield Press"). On October 25, 2001, **to bust out of the corral,** Defendant Penfield Press filed a Motion to Dismiss pursuant to Fed. R. Civ. P. 12(b)(6). For the reasons articulated below, Defendant's Motion to Dismiss shall be treated as a Motion for Summary Judgment and GRANTED IN PART.

I. FACTUAL SUMMARY

Plaintiff Barbour is the rootin'-tootin' author of _Cowboy Chow_,[1] a Texas themed cookbook containin' larapin recipes, entertainin' ideas, histooorical information, and other cowboy fun.

According to Plaintiffs, Barbour obtained a registered copyright on _Cowboy Chow_ when it was first published in 1988. Following the book's initial commercial success, there being **a lot of hungry cowpokes** out there, Barbour entered into a publishing and manufacturing agreement with Cookbook Resources on February 24, 2001, whereby Cookbook Resources acquired Barbour's copyright on _Cowboy Chow._

Sometime prior to or during 1996, an Internet magazine published by Defendant Head, called _Texas Online,_ began publishing virtually verbatim recipes from _Cowboy Chow_ without Barbour's knowledge or consent. In 1996, Defendant Penfield Press published a compilation cookbook by author Dianna Stevens ("Stevens") entitled _License to Cook Texas Style_[2] that similarly published virtually verbatim recipes from _Cowboy Chow_ without Barbour's knowledge or permission. Many of these recipes were expressly credited to Jim Head at _Texas Online._[3] After discovering these copyright infringements in May of 2001, Barbour and Cookbook Resources filed this lawsuit, specifically bringing causes of action for copyright infringement under the Copyright Act of 1976 ("Copyright Act"), 17 U.S.C. § 101 _et seq.,_ and Texas state law claims for unfair competition through misappropriation and conversion.

---

[1] It could have been named _How Now to Brown a Cow._ . . .

[2] Which could have been called _And the Cow Jumped Over the Spoon._ . . .

[3] In her affidavit, Stevens declares that she found some recipes on the Internet website, _Texas OnLine,_ and then published them in _License to Cook Texas Style_ with Head's express permission. Per Head's request, Stevens credited Jim Head and _Texas OnLine_ for each recipe obtained from _Texas OnLine._ However, Stevens claims she never saw a copy of _Cowboy Chow_ until the filing of this lawsuit. . . . The Court has previously enunciated its belief that the Internet is "one large catalyst for rumor, innuendo, and misinformation," in large part because it provides no way of verifying the authenticity of the information it presents. . . . The lawsuit aptly demonstrates that "(a)nyone

(continued)

In its Motion to Dismiss, Defendant Penfield Press seeks a dismissal of Plaintiffs' claims based on the following three grounds: (1) Plaintiffs' recipes are not copyrightable; (2) Plaintiffs' claims are barred by the applicable statutes of limitations; and (3) Plaintiffs' state law claims are preempted by federal law. Defendant also identifies approximately twenty recipes that it contends are identical, or similar, to those stated in *Cowboy Chow*.[4] Each of these recipes shares the same or a similar title, listing of ingredients, and directions for preparation, as well as sometimes employing other miscellaneous identical language.

Among the highlights from this tempting list of "cowmestibles" are "Armadillo Eggs," "Cattle Baron Cheese Dollars," "Gringo Gulch Grog," and the ever-chic "Frito Pie." In their Response, Plaintiffs refute Defendant's assertions that the alleged copied material is not copyrightable and that Plaintiffs' claims are time-barred, but concede that their state law claims properly sound in copyright and therefore are preempted by federal copyright law.

II. ANALYSIS

EDITOR'S NOTE: *The Court treated Penfield Press's Motion to Dismiss as a Motion for Summary Judgment.*

C. Copyright Infringement

Defendant contends in its Motion to Dismiss that Plaintiffs' claim for copyright infringement fails as a matter of law because cooking recipes are mere processes and procedures and therefore not copyrightable pursuant to the clear language of 17 U.S.C. § 102(b). In support of its argument, Defendant points to a letter from the Register of Copyrights stating that "mere listings of ingredients as in recipes, formulas, compounds or prescriptions are not subject to copyright protection. . . [and] [c]opyright protection does not extend to names, titles, short phrases, ideas, systems or methods." . . .

can put anything on the Internet. No website is monitored for accuracy and nothing contained therein is under oath or even subject to independent verification absent underlying documentation. . . . In short, information obtained from the Internet is "inherently untrustworthy." . . .

[4] In addition, no doubt, to being lip-smackin' good!

Defendant also relies extensively on *Publications International, Ltd. v. Meredith Corp.,* . . . a case in which the Seventh Circuit held that recipes copied from a particular compilation cookbook were not entitled to copyright protection. However, because the instant case is materially distinguishable on its facts (**with which the Court is not cowed**), and Defendant misconstrues the statement issued by the Register of Copyrights, as well as the holding in *Publications International,* **the Court ain't gonna be steered into grantin' summary judgment on this issue.**

No matter what else you herd,... to prevail on a claim of copyright infringement, a plaintiff must prove ownership of the copyrighted material and copying by the alleged infringer. . . . Copyright ownership is shown by proof of originality and copyrightability in the work as a whole and by compliance with applicable statutory formalities. . . .

However, not all copying by a defendant is actionable as copyright infringement. A copy is legally actionable only if the alleged infringer actually used the copyrighted material to create his own work, and substantial similarity exists between the two works. . . . The factual question of whether the defendant actually used the copyrighted material can be inferred by showing proof of access to the copyrighted work and probative similarity between the defendant's work and the copyrighted work. . . . In addition, not all types of work are afforded copyright protection. The Copyright Act protects original works of authorship fixed in any tangible medium of expression, ranging from literary and dramatic works to motion pictures and sound recordings. . . .

However, in no case does copyright protection extend to any idea, procedure, process, system, method of operation, concept, principle, or discovery, regardless of the form in which it is described, explained, illustrated, or embodied in such work. . . .

The Court agrees with the Defendant's assertion that the clear language of 17 U.S.C. § 102(b) denies copyright protection to mere procedures or processes. However, whether or not food recipes constitute procedures or processes ineligible for copyright protection is a question of first impression in this jurisdiction.

The Fifth Circuit has never addressed the copyrightability of food recipes, and this Court is not bound to follow the Seventh Circuit's ruling in *Publications International.* Although Defendant cites language from the Register of Copyrights indicating that recipes are uncopyrightable, this letter is not authoritative. More importantly, Defendant improperly construes the meaning of the letter by conveniently omitting the following italicized language: "Mere listings of ingredients as in recipes, formulas, compounds or prescriptions are not subject to copyright protection. **However, when a recipe or formula is accompanied by substantial literary expression in the form of an explanation or directions, or where there is a combination of recipes, as in a cookbook, there may be a basis for copyright protection.**". . . Thus, contrary to Defendant's assertion, the statement issued by the Register of Copyrights, to whatever extent it is instructive, does not declare that recipes are per se uncopyrightable.

Furthermore, even assuming *arguendo* that the Court were to adopt the Seventh Circuit's holding in *Publications International,* Defendant is incorrect in concluding that this case dictates the summary dismissal of Plaintiffs' copyright infringement claim. The claimant in *Publications International* averred that an alleged infringer had poached several recipes from its compilation cookbook entitled *Discover Dannon-50 Fabulous Recipes With Yogurt.* After carefully considering the particular characteristics and integrity of the copied material, and in light of the Supreme Court's compilation copyright jurisprudence as announced in *Feist Publication, Inc. v. Rural Tel. Serv. Co., Inc.,* . . . (holding that "white pages" telephone listings are facts unprotected by copyright law), the Seventh Circuit determined that the copied recipes consisted of nothing more than rote recitations of cooking ingredients and instructions that were therefore not sufficiently expressive to warrant copyright protection. . . . In drawing this conclusion, however, the Seventh Circuit also specifically stated: "We do not express any opinion whether recipes are or are not per se amendable to copyright protection, for it would be inappropriate to do so. The prerequisites for copyright protection necessitate case-specific inquiries, and the doctrine is not suited to broadly generalized prescriptive rules." . . .

The Court notes that the facts in the instant case are materially distinguishable from *Publications International.* First, it is unclear from the incomplete record whether or not *Publications International* and the entire compilation copyright line of cases even apply to this lawsuit. The claimant in *Publications International* owned a compilation copyright in *Discover Dannon,* as reflected by the self-declared description of the work as a "compilation" and "collective work" in its certificate of registration.[6] However, Defendant has not shown that this is also the case here. Neither Plaintiffs nor Defendant have pled or attempted to prove the type of copyright owned by Barbour and Cookbook Resources. Although *Cowboy Chow* may have been copyrighted as a compilation work, it is just as conceivable that it was registered as a literary work, given the various historical tidbits and other information that it contained. If the latter is true, the Court questions the propriety and utility of strictly applying the holdings of compilation copyright cases like *Feist* and *Publications International.*

Additionally, even if Plaintiffs' cookbook is copyrighted as a factual compilation or collective work, there still exists a genuine issue of material fact as to whether or not the copied recipes are sufficiently expressive to warrant protection under the Copyright Act. The court in *Publications International* refused to hold that recipes are unprotected as a matter of law and instead recognized that **"certain recipes may be copyrightable."**. . .

The court elaborated that recipes may warrant copyright protection in a variety of circumstances, such as where the recipe includes "suggestions for presentation, advice on wines to go with the meal, or hints on place settings with appropriate music," or where the recipes are accompanied by "tales of their historical or ethnic origin." . . . **Although the particular recipes copied from *Discover Dannon* were determined not to exhibit these types of expressions, the Court finds that there exists a genuine issue of material fact in the instant case as to whether or not the recipes**

[6] The Copyright Act defines a "compilation" as "a work formed by the collection and assembling of preexisting materials or of data that are selected, coordinated, or arranged in such a way that the resulting work as a whole constitutes an original work of authorship.". . . The term "compilation" includes collective works. A compilation copyright protects the order and manner of the presentation of the compilation's elements, but does not necessarily embrace the actual elements themselves. . . . The only expression entitled to copyright protection, then, is the manner in which the compiler has selected and arranged the facts.

procured from *Cowboy Chow* represent mere unprotected facts or actual protected expression.

Of the twenty recipes identified in Defendant's Motion as being identical or similar, the Court finds that at least a few contain statements that may be sufficiently expressive to exceed the boundaries of mere fact. Unlike its counterparts in *Publications International,* the recipes in *Cowboy Chow* are infused with light-hearted or helpful commentary, some of which also appears verbatim in *License to Cook Texas Style.*

For example, the *Cowboy Chow* recipe for "Cherokee Chicken" states in part: "Heat oil in heavy skillet. Add sugar and let it brown and bubble. (This is the secret to the unique taste!)" The virtually identical recipe in *License to Cook Texas Style* mimics this parenthetical and arguably expressive language, excepting the exclamation point: "Heat oil in heavy skillet. Add sugar and let it brown and bubble (this is the secret to the unique taste)." Similarly oriented anecdotal language also appears in recipes for "Crazy Horse Cranberry Sauce with Raisins," (stating **"Great with all your meats!"** in *Cowboy Chow* as compared to **"Great with meats!"** in *License to Cook Texas Style*), as well as "Pico de Gallo" (**translating "Pico de Gallo" as "Beak of the Rooster" in both books**). In other instances, Barbour's suggestions on the presentation of food also appear in Defendant's book. **For example, both cookbooks suggest using the "Frito" bag as a bowl for eating "Frito Pie," serving "Prairie Fire Dip" hot in a chafing dish, and filling a "glass cowboy boot mug" with "Red Beer."** Based on this small sample of recipes alone, the Court cannot conclude as a matter of law that the material allegedly copied from *Cowboy Chow* is nothing more than mere recitations of facts that are not entitled to copyright protection. **Barbour's recipes contain more than mechanical listings of ingredients and cooking directions, and as such, the Court will not grant summary judgment in favor of Defendant on the unqualified notion that recipes are uncopyrightable.**

D. Statute of Limitations

Penfield Press also seeks summary judgment on the basis that Plaintiffs' claims are time-barred. Specifically, Defendant argues that because Plaintiffs' state and federal law causes of action began accruing when

License to Cook Texas Style was first published in 1996, Plaintiffs' claims for unfair competition through misappropriation, conversion, and copyright infringement are barred by the applicable two- and three-year statutes of limitations. In contrast, Plaintiffs contend that these claims did not commence accruing until Barbour first discovered the copyright violations in May of 2001. Plaintiffs further argue that irrespective of the accrual date, they may still recover for damages accumulated three years prior to the filing of the suit. Because the Court dismisses Plaintiffs' state law claims below on federal preemption grounds, it need only address the timeliness of Plaintiffs' copyright infringement action.

Civil actions brought under the Copyright Act must commence within three years from the time the claim accrues. . . . Thus, the material inquiry in the present case is exactly when Plaintiffs' claim against Penfield Press accrued. Plaintiff asserts, and the Court concurs, that nothing in the law of the Fifth Circuit forecloses the application of the discovery rule or any other equitable tolling rules to copyright infringement actions. In *Daboub v. Gibbons,* . . . the Fifth Circuit determined that the plaintiffs' copyright infringement claim was time-barred because they either actually or constructively knew of the defendants' infringing conduct four years prior to bringing suit. Although never explicitly stated, the court in *Daboub* impliedly accepted the underlying assertion that the discovery rule applied in the context of copyright infringement claims.[7] . . . Furthermore, in *Prather v. Neva Paperbacks, Inc.,* . . . the Fifth Circuit unequivocally stated that general equitable tolling doctrines apply to copyright infringement actions (applying the equitable doctrine of fraudulent concealment). . . . Based on this precedent, the Court finds that general equitable tolling doctrines, including the discovery rule, apply to Plaintiffs' copyright infringement claim.

Having determined that general equitable tolling principles apply, the Court cannot hold that Plaintiffs' claims are time-barred as a matter of law. In the instant case, Plaintiffs allege, and Penfield Press does not dispute, that Plaintiffs only discovered Defendant's infringing conduct

---

[7] Specifically, the Daboub court noted that the discovery rule did not apply to certain of the plaintiffs' state law causes of action, but proceeded to apply the discovery rule to the plaintiffs' remaining claims, including one brought under the Copyright Act.

when Barbour happened upon a copy of *License to Cook Texas Style* in a bookstore in Bandera, Texas, in May of 2001. Accepting this uncontroverted fact as true, then, Plaintiffs' cause of action arguably did not accrue until Barbour first discovered Defendant's book in May of this year.[8] However, even if Defendant is correct that Plaintiffs' claim began accruing at the time *License to Cook Texas Style* was published in 1996, it is well established that the three-year limitations period bars only the remedy, not the substantive right. . . .

("[T]he intent of the drafters was that the limitations period would affect the remedy only, not the substantive right, and that equitable considerations would therefore apply to suspend the running of the statute.") Because Penfield Press has not proved that Plaintiffs' cause of action accrued prior to May of 2001, the Court cannot grant summary judgment on the ground that Plaintiffs' federal claim is time-barred.

E. State Law Claims

Finally, Defendant argues that Plaintiffs' state law claims for unfair competition through misappropriation and conversion are preempted by federal copyright law and therefore subject to dismissal. **Takin' the bull by its cooked horns,** Plaintiffs concede that their state law claims properly sound in copyright, but explain that these claims were brought as "insurance" against the dismissal of their federal cause of action. Although the Court appreciates Plaintiffs' all-inclusive approach, Plaintiffs' state law claims are clearly preempted by federal law. The Copyright Act stipulates that it exclusively governs all legal and equitable rights falling within the general scope and subject matter of copyright, such that "no person is entitled to any such right or equivalent right in any such work under the common law or statues of any State." . . . Because Plaintiffs in this case

---

[8] The Court is aware that the recordation of a document in the Copyright Office may provide constructive notice of the work. . . . However, Penfield Press never raises this argument in its Motion nor provides any evidence that *License to Cook Texas Style* was properly registered in the Copyright Office in accordance with the statute in 1996. Additionally, even if such evidence were provided, the Court notes that other equitable considerations might still operate to toll the limitations period.

30—

admit that their state law claims sound in copyright, the Court need not elaborate on this issue any further.

The Court finds that Plaintiffs' state law claims for unfair competition through misappropriation and conversion are preempted by federal copyright law, and therefore GRANTS summary judgment in favor of Defendant on this issue *only,* and DISMISSES Plaintiffs' state law claims *only.*

III. CONCLUSION

For all of the reasons set forth above, Defendant Penfield Press's Motion to Dismiss, treated as a Motion for Summary Judgment, is hereby GRANTED IN PART. The Court specifically DENIES summary judgment on the issues relating to Plaintiffs' copyright infringement claim, and GRANTS summary judgment on the issues of Federal preemption *only.* Because Plaintiffs' state law claims are preempted by federal law, the Court hereby DISMISSES Plaintiffs' claims arising under Texas state law for unfair competition through misappropriation and conversion *only.* A final judgment regarding such will be entered in due course.

IT IS SO ORDERED DONE this 21st day of December, 2001 at Galveston, Texas.

Signature
SAMUEL B. KENT
UNITED STATES DISTRICT JUDGE

ON A WING AND A PRAYER
Carol Blakely of Dallas
Flies to the Rescue

AND WHO IN THE WORLD IS CAROL?

- A native Texan and cook extraordinaire
- A culinary historian • A computer expert
- A feisty grandmother

A former systems consultant for a software company, Carol shares her love of cooking with her retired military husband, Ralph, their three adult children, and five grandchildren. She also runs The Jalapeño Café, *www.jalapenocafe.com, a website with monthly recipe updates and a cooking newsletter with subscribers from around the world.*

I DON'T HAVE A DOG IN THIS HUNT, OR DO I?

By Carol Blakely

It all started back in March 2001 with an e-mail from Maureen Patterson of Penfield Press. Penfield Press was getting ready to reprint the cookbook *License to Cook Arizona Style.* My website, *The Jalapeño Café,* had contributed recipes to the last printing in 1999. Maureen wanted to know if the recipes could be used again, and if they needed updating before reprinting.

(In case I haven't mentioned it, I am a serious "foodie" and cookbook collector. My favorite type of cuisine is Southwestern and I have a recipe website devoted to Southwestern cuisine and culture. I have a large library of Southwestern, Mexican, and Texas cookbooks.) Later, I received an e-mail from Joan Liffring-Zug Bourret, who mentioned that Penfield Press had to revise another of their cookbooks, *License to Cook Texas Style*, because they were being sued over the use of some of the recipes in the book. Joan suggested I go to their website and read the legal filings.

When I read the Penfield Press web pages, I felt like I was on another planet. Joan faxed copies of the recipes in question to me. I read familiar names as I flipped through the pages: Pico de Gallo, Black-Eyed Pea Dip, Buttermilk Pie, Cheese Dollars, Red Velvet Cake, Frito™ Pie, Guacamole, Margaritas, Margarita Pie, Sopapillas, and Texas Trash™.

These recipes are old Texas favorites. Reviewing the titles brought these thoughts to my mind. Pico de Gallo? Baloney! — AND DOESN'T ALMOST EVERY MEXICAN RESTAURANT "HAVE" this relish on the menu? Black-Eyed Pea Dip? Helen Corbitt published this recipe in the 1950s. Margarita Pie? This dish was on the menu at Mariano's Restaurant in Arlington, Texas, in the 1970s. Red Velvet Cake? This recipe and its variations go back sixty years. Buttermilk Pie? My granny baked this pie for every special occasion. Frito™ Pie in the bag? A standard at Friday night football games from El Paso to Texarkana. Guacamole? This food was documented when Cortez invaded Mexico over five hundred years ago. Frozen Margaritas made with limeade concentrate? A staple of backyard barbeques for years. Texas Trash™? Didn't the Wheat Chex™ people come up with this recipe and its similar versions over fifty years ago?

I sat down on the floor in front of my bookshelf and started going though my cookbooks, comparing the recipes to the ones faxed to me. I found the titles of the "lawsuit" recipes listed in my cookbooks repeatedly. Maybe the ingredients or measurement weren't exactly the same — *Cowboy Chow's* recipe for buttermilk pie called for five eggs instead of three, adding chopped green onions to guacamole, and serving Red Eye beer in a glass boot. Glass boots for drinks were popular in years past. And talk about similarities, *Cowboy Chow's* recipe for sopapillas stated, "Cook only several pieces at a time, turning once so they will puff up easily," while one of my cookbooks (*Texas on the Half Shell*, published five years before *Cowboy Chow*) said, "Cook only several pieces at a time, turning once so they will puff up evenly."

My good ole boy husband came in and asked why I was so concerned with this matter. "You don't have a dog in this hunt," he said. But he was wrong: I did have a "dog in this hunt." My cooking website has over five hundred recipes listed, many sent to me from readers. There is no way for me to know the origin of all these recipes. If Penfield Press could be sued, it could happen to me, or to take this thought a little further, it could happen to any church, school, or civic organization that sells compilation cookbooks.

In my opinion, it's true that Texans like to sue; the courthouse battle has replaced the gun battle of Wild West days. I am not opposed to having your day in court, but some subjects should never see the light of day in a courtroom, and one is recipes. If you spend hours in the kitchen creating a dish, using commonly available ingredients, chances are that someone, somewhere has already tried the same thing, told her friend about it, who in turn tried the recipe, changed a few measurements, and claimed it as her own. In addition, it is a common practice to add comments like, "it goes well with chicken" or "this was my grandmother's recipe" or "great with meats."

Furthermore, compilation cookbooks follow a long tradition of swapping and trading recipes with the same recipes showing up over and over again. This is how the history of regional foods is created. Even some commercially developed recipes, such as Red Velvet Cake and Wheat Chex's Snack Mix™ (called "Trash" in Texas) have moved into the realm of American food lore.

Recipes are about who we are, where we come from, and are part of the history and traditions of our country. Claiming ownership to a certain recipe is like laying claim to the custom of putting out cookies for Santa Claus. Should one person claim to own the rights to this custom?

Recipes are part of our tradition, too. They are treasured and handed down from mother to daughter, from friend to neighbor, along with comments and stories that make the recipes more interesting. All of this information builds into one large pool of cooking knowledge to be shared by all, just as any family ought to be able to put out that plate of cookies on Christmas Eve. I found this idea for sharing in an old community cookbook.

"An unshared recipe will soon be forgotten, but a shared recipe will live forever."

Kelly Fields, San Antonio
Aviators inspecting new aeroplane

THE RECIPES CITED FOR VIOLATING COPYRIGHT OF *COWBOY CHOW*

License to Cook Texas Style has 116 recipes while *Cowboy Chow* has 151 recipes.

Cookbook Tip

While titles are not copyrightable, names such as Texas Trash™ and Frito™ Pie are trademarked. It is difficult to know if a trademark is needed when publishing the name of an ingredient without checking to see if a trademark symbol is used on the packaging for the ingredient. Note the number of trademarks for common ingredients in the recipe section of this book. Trademarks rather than copyrights protect the product identity of food manufacturers.

THE INTERNET RECIPE PANTRY

Penfield's defense lawyers requested, "Find recipes published prior to 1988 duplicating or with similar comments of expression as the recipes cited in the lawsuit." Facts from the Internet food pantry were compiled by Jordan Heusinkveld, the publisher's teenage grandson. He found thousands of recipes tantalizingly close in many ways to those in *Cowboy Chow*. Here is a sample of the titles of recipes found on the Internet. All listed below have almost 1,000 entries or more.

APPETIZERS, DIPS, AND SALSA

Armadillo Eggs was featured in dozens of pages with more about armadillos than you ever hoped to know, plus recipes from cooks with books and restaurants featured on websites.

Black-eyed Pea Dip

Cattle Baron Cheese Dollars

Guacamole appeared to be most popular.

Pico de Gallo

Prairie Fire Dip

Tex-Chex Mix

MAIN DISHES

Crazy Horse Cranberry Sauce with Raisins brings forth many recipes along with entries about Chief Crazy Horse.

Frito™ **Pie**

Cherokee Chicken has a title linking the dish to the Cherokee Native Americans who wrote that chicken was not an early American dish.

DESSERTS

Red Velvet Cake
Margarita Pie
Sopapillas

THE SALOON

Margaritas
Texas Peach Fuzzies

It would take the major part of a lifetime to examine each of these recipes and sources for similarities and duplications of the recipes cited in the lawsuit. Troubling to Penfield Press was that for many months during 2001–2002, similar recipes to those in *Cowboy Chow* remained on the Internet, migrating to a variety of sites; yet, Penfield Press faced a lawsuit potentially costing thousands of dollars in fines and legal fees for similar recipes.

U. S. POST OFFICE AND COURT HOUSE, TEXARKANA, ARK.-TEX.

UNITED·STATES POST·OFFICE·AND COURT·HOUSE

© OTTO MOORE

TEXARKANA, TEXAS   TEXARKANA, ARKANSAS
MAN IN ARKANSAS AND HIS ASS IN TEXAS

RESEARCH, RECIPES, AND ESSAYS
by
CAROL BLAKELY

Carol Blakely is shown with several of the Texas recipe books in her vast collection, many of them critical evidence in the lawsuit. She likes to cite the blessing below in times of stress.

An Old Gaelic Blessing

May the roads rise with you
And the wind be always at your back
And may the Lord hold you
in the hollow of his hand.

CAROL BLAKELY'S RESEARCH

Carol Blakely researched 105 Texas cookbooks published prior to 1988, of which 35 contained variations or, in some cases, virtually verbatim sections duplicating traditional Texas recipes similar to those cited in the *Cowboy Chow* lawsuit. Recipe origins link to many lands, including those from Africa to the Caribbean to Texas. She shares information about the recipes and her updated favorites in the succeeding pages of this book. She also collected charming sayings from historic Texas cookbooks. Following is a list of her major bibliography.

RECIPE	COOKBOOK	YR. PUB.	PAGE(s)
Armadillo Eggs	More Calf Fries to Caviar	1988	119
	Eyes of Texas Cookbook	1987	13
Black-Eyed Pea Dip	Helen Corbitt Cookbook	1957	13
	The Only Texas Cookbook	1981	5
	Gingerbread and All the Trimmings	1987	8
	Tastes and Tales from Texas	1984	3, 110
	Lone Star Legacy	1981	298
	The Texas Experience	1982	14
	Texas on the Half Shell	1982	156
	A Texas Hill Country Cookbook	1976	348
	Seasoned with the Sun	1974	202
	The Texas Cookbook	1965	472
	Hullabaloo in the Kitchen–Aggie Moms	1983	111
Buttermilk Pie	What's Cookin' in Abilene	1984	7
	Texas on the Half Shell	1982	222
	A Texas Hill Country Cookbook	1975	257
	Through Our Kitchen Door (2 recipes)	1978	175
	A Little Bit of Texas Cooking	1988	198
	What's on the Menu?	1946	82
	Wide, Wide World of Texas Cooking	1970	355
	The Texas Experience	1982	58
	The Only Texas Cookbook	1981	224
	Gingerbread and All the Trimmings	1987	211
	Tastes and Tales from Texas	1984	156
	Texas Celebrity Cookbook	1984	180
	Calf Fries to Caviar	1983	231
	The Eyes of Texas Cookbook	1987	221
	Lone Star Legacy	1981	258
	Houston Junior League Cookbook	1968	354
	What's Cooking in Tyler	1980	87, 88
	What's Cooking in Texas (9 recipes)	1986	255, 258

RECIPE	COOKBOOK	YR. PUB.	PAGE(s)
Cheese Dollars	Our Daily Bread	1984	2
	A Texas Hill Country Cookbook	1976	15
	Through Our Kitchen Door–Dallas	1978	23
	A Little Bit of Texas Cooking	1988	94
	Seasoned with the Sun–El Paso	1974	24
	The Texas Cookbook	1965	265
	A Taste of Texas (2 recipes)	1949	20, 21
	West Coast Cookbook	1952	4
	Houston Junior League Cookbook	1968	13
	What's Cooking in Tyler	1980	3
	Hullabaloo in the Kitchen–Aggie Moms	1986	125
Cherokee Chicken	(Research found elsewhere.)		
Cranberry Sauce with Raisins	Houston Junior League Cookbook	1968	275
Diamond Lil's Red Velvet Cake w/Icing	More Calf Fries to Caviar	1988	194
	Kitchen Kookery	1967	117
	Hullabaloo in the Kitchen–Aggie Moms	1983	74
	Angel Food (Dallas)	1987	102
	What's Cooking in Texas	1986	150
	Favorite Recipes of the Vocal Majority (Dallas)	1978	48
El Vacquero Coffee	Mexican Family Favorites Cook Book	1983	118
Frito™ Pie	A Little Bit of Texas Cooking	1988	94
	Jane Butel's Tex-Mex Cook Book	1980	116
	Kitchen Kookery (Dallas)	1967	7
	A Taste of Texas	1949	169
	What's on the Menu? (Dallas)	1946	55
	What's Cooking in Tyler?	1980	48
Gringo Gulch Grog	A Little Bit of Texas Cooking	1988	9
Guacamole	Texas on the Half Shell	1982	95
	Sandoval's Mexican Cookbook	1966	20
	Mexican Border Book	1973	14
	Our Daily Bread	1984	18
	A Texas Hill Country Cookbook	1976	324
	A Little Bit of Texas Cooking	1988	103, 259
	Seasoned with the Sun–El Paso	1974	16
	The Texas Cookbook	1965	223
	Wide, Wide World of Texas Cooking	1970	102
	The Texas Experience	1982	13
	The Only Texas Cookbook	1981	92
	The World of Mexican Cooking	1971	20
	The Eyes of Texas Cookbook	1987	107

RECIPE	COOKBOOK	YR. PUB.	PAGE(s)
	Creative Mexican Cooking	1985	112
	Lone Star Legacy	1981	12
	A Taste of Texas	1949	165
	Taste and Tales of Texas	1984	110
	What's Cooking in Tyler?	1980	5
	Our Favorite Mexican Recipes–Del Rio	1982	3
	The Avocado Bravo Avocado Growers Cookbook	1970	35
	Calf Fries to Caviar	1983	34
	More Calf Fries to Caviar	1988	162
	Jane Butel's Tex-Mex Cookbook	1980	34
	Lone Star Legacy	1981	45
Margarita Pie	Texas on the Half Shell	1982	137
	Hullabaloo in the Kitchen–Aggie Moms	1983	134
	All Faiths Receiving Home Auxiliary Cookbook–Albuquerque, New Mexico	1980	66
Pico de Gallo	Texas on the Half Shell	1982	98
	A Little Bit of Texas Cooking	1988	102
	Seasoned with the Sun–El Paso Jr. League	1974	212
	Gingerbread and All the Trimmings Waxahachie, Texas	1987	13
	Texas Celebrity Cookbook	1984	233
	Our Favorite Mexican Recipes–Del Rio	1982	12
	More Calf Fries to Caviar	1988	167
	Creative Mexican Cooking	1985	40
	The Eyes of Texas Cookbook	1987	125
Prairie Fire Dip	Texas on the Half Shell	1982	158
	Our Daily Bread	1984	5
	A Hill Country Cookbook	1976	348
	Seasoned with the Sun–El Paso Jr. League	1974	14
	Wide, Wide World of Texas Cooking	1970	239
	Taste and Tales of Texas	1984	8
	Our Favorite Mexican Recipes–Del Rio	1982	2
	The World of Mexican Cooking	1971	32
	Calf Fries to Caviar	1988	12
	Jane Butel's Tex-Mex Cookbook	1980	28
	The Eyes of Texas Cookbook	1987	11
	Lone Star Legacy	11986	14
	Cookbook–Everman, Texas	1981	4
	Angel Food (Dallas)	1987	1
	Helen Corbitt Cookbook	1957	11
	Houston Jr. League Cook Book	1968	8

RECIPE	COOKBOOK	YR. PUB.	PAGE(s)
Sopapillas	Texas on the Half Shell	1982	133
	Mexican Border Cookbook	1973	37
	A Texas Hill Country Cookbook	1976	330
	Through Our Kitchen Door (Dallas)	1978	164
	Seasoned with the Sun–El Paso Jr. League	1974	57
	Gingerbread and All the Trimmings Waxahachie, Texas	1987	247
	Our Favorite Mexican Recipes–Del Rio	1982	49
	Calf Fries to Caviar	1983	185
	More Calf Fries to Caviar	1988	188
	Houston Jr. League Cookbook	1968	213
	Cooking with the AAMA–Dallas	1979	35
Texas Caviar	The Bounty of East Texas	1977	32
	Wide, Wide World of Texas Cooking	1970	239
	More Calf Fries to Caviar	1988	10
	Eyes of Texas Cookbook	1987	51
	Through Our Kitchen Door (Dallas)	1978	18
	Favorite Recipes of the Vocal Majority (Dallas)	1978	1
Texas Trash™	What's Cookin' in Abilene?	1984	7
	Texas on the Half Shell	1982	157
	Our Daily Bread	1984	122
	Calf Fries to Caviar	1983	29
	More Calf Fries to Caviar	1988	10
	Kitchen Kookery (Dallas)	1967	7
	What's Cooking in Tyler?	1980	5
	The Eyes of Texas Cookbook	1987	12
	Westphalia Cookbook	1980	4
	Hullabaloo in the Kitchen–Aggie Moms	1983	347
Texas Peach Fuzzies	The Texas Experience	1982	103
	Jane Butel's Tex-Mex Cookbook	1980	37
	Hullabaloo in the Kitchen–Aggie Moms	1983	133

EDITOR'S NOTE: *We ultimately needed to prove by example that the recipes involved in the suit against Penfield Press were commonly used in many cookbooks.* *For instance, one of our Penfield Press authors, Gerry Kangas of Aurora, Minnesota, found a very similar cake icing in a 1960s women's club cookbook.*

CAROL BLAKELY'S RECIPES

LITTLE WHIMS
(APPETIZERS)

PICO DE GALLO

Pico de Gallo (Rooster's Beak) is the name for a common Mexican table relish. The name comes from the fact that the relish is hot and will "peck" when eaten. In the southern part of Mexico, it is made with oranges, jicama, and chili powder. The jicama is a crunchy root vegetable that tastes like a cross between a potato and an apple. In Northern Mexico, in the cattle-raising states, Pico de Gallo is made with tomatoes, onions, and jalapeño peppers. The Northern version is a popular accompaniment to fajitas. Here are recipes for the two versions of Pico de Gallo and one for Easy Skillet Fajitas.

Pico de Gallo One (Rooster's Beak)

3 cups chopped jicama
2 cups chopped oranges
2 limes, juiced
Salt to taste
Piquin chili powder to taste
   (or any hot chili powder)

Limes

Combine the jicama and orange. Add the lime juice and salt to taste. Mix well; chill for 2 to 3 hours. Just before serving sprinkle lightly with the chili powder.

Pico de Gallo Two (Rooster's Beak)

4 or 5 ripe plum or Roma tomatoes, finely chopped
1 small onion, finely chopped
1/4 cup fresh, chopped cilantro
2 or 3 fresh jalapeños, chopped
    (for less heat, remove seeds and white membranes)
Juice of 2 limes
1 teaspoon salt

Mix ingredients and chill for 1 hour before serving.

Easy Skillet Fajitas

4 chicken breast halves
Juice of 2 limes
2 teaspoons garlic powder
4 tablespoons Worcestershire sauce
2 tablespoons salad or olive oil
1 large onion, sliced in rounds
1 large bell pepper, top and membrane removed, sliced in rings
Salt and pepper to taste

Trim fat from chicken and slice lengthwise into thin pieces. Mix lime juice, garlic powder, Worcestershire sauce, and oil; pour over chicken, coating well. Let stand 15 to 20 minutes. Heat heavy skillet and spray with nonstick spray. Remove chicken from marinade and place on hot skillet to cook. Add the sliced vegetables to the leftover marinade to soak while the chicken cooks. Turn chicken to ensure it is cooked throughout, 6 to 8 minutes. Add the vegetables and cook a few minutes more. Season with salt and pepper. Heap on hot platter to serve. Serve with hot flour tortillas, Pico de Gallo, sour cream, guacamole, refried beans, and lime slices.

Easy way to heat tortillas: Lay eight tortillas flat and wrap paper towels around them. Microwave on high for 60 seconds. Let stand a minute to finish heating through.

PRAIRIE FIRE

In Mexican culture, serving *anjojitos* (little whims) or appetizers before a meal is a long-standing tradition. This custom is why you are served corn chips and salsa in a Mexican restaurant while waiting for your meal. Some popular Mexican foods in America derived from *anjojitos* are nachos, chile con queso, and tacos. Serving mashed beans as *anjojitos* is documented in Josefina Velazquez de Leon's 1948 cookbook *Mexican Cook Book Devoted to American Homes.*

I found a Prairie Fire recipe in a Gonzales, Texas, cookbook, *Tried and True Cook Book,* from the Women's Society of Christian Service, published in 1955. This recipe has two strong similarities to the Prairie Fire recipe in *Cowboy Chow.* It calls for Ranch-Style Beans™, a chili-flavored pinto bean product, long popular in Texas, and it recommends serving in a chafing dish with chips. In her popular 1957 book *Helen Corbitt's Cook Book,* Miss Corbitt included the Prairie Fire recipe. After that, the recipe was quickly adopted by Texas cooks and started showing up in almost every community cookbook. It is a great-tasting dish and easy to prepare. Here are two versions, one with Ranch-Style Beans™ and one using canned refried beans.

FORT WORTH LIVE STOCK EXCHANGE, FT. WORTH, TEXAS

Prairie Fire One

4 tablespoons butter
1 onion, finely grated
1 garlic clove, finely minced
1 can Ranch-Style Beans™ (or chili beans)
2 pickled jalapeño peppers, minced,
    plus 2 or 3 tablespoons of the jalapeño juice
1 cup grated Cheddar cheese

Peppers

Melt butter in skillet. Add onion and cook until limp. Add garlic and cook 1 minute longer, then add beans. Mash beans with potato masher as they cook. Add the jalapeños and juice, mixing well. Turn heat to low and add cheese, stirring to melt. Serve the dip in a chafing dish with tortilla chips.

Prairie Fire Two

1 can refried beans
1 (4-ounce) can chopped green chilies
1 teaspoon garlic salt
1/4 cup butter
2 pickled jalapeños, minced
1 cup grated Cheddar cheese

Place refried beans, green chilies, garlic salt, butter, and jalapeños in heavy pan or skillet and cook on medium heat until warm, adding a little water if needed. Turn heat to low and add cheese, stirring to mix. Serve with tortilla chips.

Note: This recipe can be made in the microwave, covering the first mixture with waxed paper and cooking on high 3 minutes, then stirring and cooking 2 minutes more. Add cheese and cook on low 1 minute.

CHEESE DOLLARS

The earliest version of this recipe that I found was in a 1952 cookbook, *West Coast Cookbook*. In this book, it is called "Cheese Coins." Cheese wafer recipes have been around for many years, and almost every community cookbook will have at least one version. When Lyndon Johnson was president in the 1960s, his wife, Lady Bird, was generous in sharing her favorite recipes with the public. Her recipe for these cheese crackers calls for adding Rice Krispies™ for extra crunch.

The disputed Cheese Dollar recipe in *Cowboy Chow* calls for placing a dab of jalapeño jelly in the center of each cracker. Other toppings are pecan halves, date bits, or a few caraway seeds. It is up to the maker to find a favorite topping.

Here are two versions of the Cheese Dollar crackers: Lady Bird Johnson's recipe and one that uses pecan halves in the center.

Lady Bird Johnson's Cheese Wafers

2 sticks (1 cup) butter
1 pound sharp Cheddar cheese, grated
1 teaspoon cayenne pepper
Dash of salt
2 cups flour
2 cups plain Rice Krispies™

Place butter in bowl and mix with grated cheese to soften at room temperature. When softened, add cayenne and salt to flour. Add flour mixture to cheese mixture. This can be done with a food processor or mixer, but add Rice Krispies™ by hand. Drop by small rounds on a greased cookie sheet. Press with the back of the spoon to flatten. Bake at 350° for 10 to 12 minutes until lightly browned. Makes 60 wafers.

Old-fashioned Cheese Dollars

1/2 cup butter
1 cup grated sharp Cheddar cheese
2 (3-ounce) packages cream cheese, softened
2-1/4 cups flour
1 teaspoon cayenne pepper
1/8 teaspoon salt
1 teaspoon white pepper
Pecan halves

Cream butter and cheeses together until cheese is thoroughly incorporated. Mix in remaining ingredients. Divide dough into two equal parts and shape each part into a long roll about 2 inches across. Wrap rolls in waxed paper and chill until firm (2 hours or more). To bake, slice into 1/4-inch-thick rounds and place on ungreased cookie sheet. Press a pecan half in the center of each "dollar."

Bake in 350° oven 10 to 12 minutes until lightly browned. Makes 70 to 80. These wafers store well in an airtight container.

Cactus in Bloom, San Antonio, Texas.

ARMADILLO EGGS

I first read about this recipe in a cooking column in the local newspaper, sometime in the early 1980s. After that, I noticed the recipe in two Texas cookbooks, *More Calf Fries to Caviar*, 1988, and *Eyes of Texas Cookbook*, 1987. Then, while researching the recipes cited in the lawsuit, I remembered that I had a similar recipe called Poo Poos given to me when I lived in San Antonio back in the 1960s. I made this recipe a few times, then tucked it away in my files and forgot about it. This recipe calls for Bisquick™, grated cheese, sausage, and jalapeños, which are major ingredients in Armadillo Eggs. I'll let you be the judge. Here are the recipes for Poo Poos and *The Jalapeño Café*'s recipe for Armadillo Eggs.

Poo Poos

12 ounces sharp Cheddar cheese, grated
1 pound pork sausage (hot preferred)
3 cups Bisquick™
2 tablespoons finely chopped, pickled jalapeños

Put ingredients in bowl and let stand 15 or 20 minutes to reach room temperature. Mix thoroughly by hand. Allow the mixture to rest for 15 to 20 minutes. Form the dough into 1-inch balls. Place on an ungreased cookie sheet and bake in 350° oven 10 to 12 minutes until lightly browned. Yield will be about 100 Poo Poos.

Armadillo Eggs

2 cups Bisquick™
1 pound bulk sausage (room temperature)
2 cups shredded Cheddar cheese
2 jars whole jalapeño peppers
1 cup shredded Monterey Jack cheese
1 package Shake 'N Bake™ for Pork

Mix Bisquick™, sausage, and Cheddar cheese by hand. Remove stems from peppers and slice lengthwise. Stuff the peppers with the Monterey Jack cheese. Pat small pieces of the Bisquick™ mixture flat and wrap around the stuffed peppers.

Roll each one in the Shake 'N Bake™. Place on ungreased cookie sheet and bake at 425° for 15 to 20 minutes. Makes 20 to 30 "eggs."

A POOR TEXAN...
© CURT TEICH & CO., INC.

GUACAMOLE

The avocado tree originated in the Tehuacan Valley of Southern Mexico, and by the time Cortez and his conquistadors invaded Mexico in 1521, it was cultivated throughout Latin America. A Spanish priest and historian who accompanied Cortez wrote about a dish called Ahuacatl. According to the priest, it was prepared with avocados, tomatoes, and chilies and was Montezuma's favorite food. So, the next time guacamole is served at your favorite Mexican restaurant, remember, you are eating an ancient dish once served to a king!

Over the years, I have made guacamole hundreds of times and used many different recipes. Almost all were good, but I have come to some conclusions about guacamole. The basic ingredients that must be in guacamole (besides the avocado) are tomato, garlic, salt, and lime juice. I like to use fresh garlic, but have used garlic powder in a pinch. The addition of any type of green chile is good, as well as onion and cilantro.

If I am serving the guacamole with a main course, I make it plain with only the basic ingredients. If is going to be eaten as a dip, I like to add extra ingredients to give it more texture and flavor.

The old story about placing the seed in the dish to keep the avocado from turning brown is simply not true. The only way to keep leftover guacamole from darkening is to squeeze a little lemon or lime juice over the top of the mixture, then cover and store in the refrigerator. It will be green the next day.

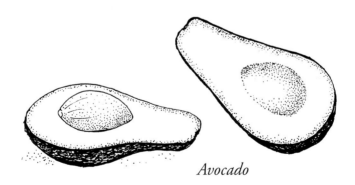

Avocado

Here are two recipes that I have used many times. Perfect Guacamole is my main-course favorite.

Perfect Guacamole

2 large or 3 medium-sized ripe avocados, peeled and deseeded
1 small ripe plum tomato
1 or 2 cloves of garlic, mashed
1 teaspoon salt or salt to taste
Juice of 1 lime combined with the salt

Mash avocado with fork until almost smooth, leaving a few lumps for texture. Slice the end off the tomato and grate the pulp into the avocado mixture; discard the tomato skin. Add the mashed garlic and salt/lime juice, mixing well. Chill in the refrigerator 15 to 20 minutes before serving.

Guacamole Dip

3 or 4 large ripe avocados, peeled and deseeded
1 small ripe tomato, peeled and finely chopped
1 (4-ounce) can chopped green chilies
1 pickled jalapeño, finely chopped (for heat lovers only)
2 tablespoons finely chopped onion
1 or 2 garlic cloves, mashed with 1 teaspoon of salt
Juice of 1 lime

Place avocados in bowl and mash with fork until almost smooth. Leave a few lumps for texture. Add the other ingredients and mix well. Serve at once with corn tortilla chips.

Tomato

TEXAS CAVIAR

Some confusion exists over this recipe. In Helen Corbitt's 1957 cookbook, she published her pickled black-eyed pea dip, which was later named "Texas Caviar." Now, Texas Caviar recipes show up in two forms: the olive-tomato mixture similar to the one in *Cowboy Chow* and the pickled black-eyed pea dip made popular by Helen Corbitt. The recipe for the olive version is also called Cowboy Caviar. (I didn't name it, just read it that way.) The earliest example that I found for the black olive-based recipe was in the 1970 cookbook *The Wide, Wide World of Texas Cooking*. It is also listed in the 1978 cookbook *Through Our Kitchen Door,* from the Dallas, Texas Historical Society.

The olive mixture is similar to Creole Black Olive Salad, which is used when making New Orleans' famous sandwich, the Muffletta.

Here is a recipe for a black olive and green bean salad that has all the flavors of Texas Caviar, plus the taste of Texas sweet onions.

Texas Caviar (with black olives)

1 pound fresh green beans
2 ripe tomatoes, chopped
1 can whole ripe black olives (without seeds)
1 Texas sweet onion (Noonday or 1015 preferred), cut into rings

Dressing:
3/4 cup extra-virgin olive oil
3 tablespoons lemon juice
2 cloves garlic, finely minced
1 teaspoon Dijon mustard
1 teaspoon salt
1/2 teaspoon fresh cracked pepper

Clean beans, removing stems and ends. Cook about 5 minutes in salted boiling water. Drain and place in ice water to stop cooking. When cool, drain and chill until ready to use.

To make salad, place green beans, tomatoes, olives, and onion in large bowl. Mix dressing ingredients and pour over salad. Toss lightly to mix and chill about 15 minutes before serving. Great with fried chicken and barbeque.

BLACK-EYED PEA DIP

Helen Corbitt first documented this recipe in her popular 1957 cookbook *Helen Corbitt's Cookbook.* Corbitt, a New Yorker, came to Texas in the 1930s and worked in Austin and Houston before moving to Dallas, where her delicious recipes put Neiman Marcus's Zodiac Room restaurant on the map. In the early 1950s, the economy was booming and Texans were putting the Depression and war years behind them, striving for the finer life. Helen Corbitt was the Grande Dame of Texas cooking, and she brought the lowly legume into the cocktail circuit by creating a dish she called Pickled Black-Eyed Peas, a mixture of cooked peas and onions in a vinaigrette dressing. She says in the 1957 book, "I serve few parties at any time of the year without them. And the men, how they love them!"

Since then, untold versions of this recipe have been published in Texas cookbooks. It has been called Black-Eyed Pea Dip, Pickled Black-Eyed Peas, and Texas Caviar. A black-eyed pea dish is a must for New Year's Day football parties, for every good Texan (and southerner) knows you must eat black-eyed peas on New Year's Day for good luck in the coming year. Here is a version of a black-eyed pea dip that can double as a salad and is perfect for New Year's Day.

Black-Eyed Pea Dip or Salad

2 (16-ounce) cans black-eyed peas, drained
1 small onion, diced
2 ripe plum tomatoes, chopped
1 green (or red) bell pepper, diced
3 or 4 stalks celery, finely diced
2 to 3 tablespoons finely chopped jalapeño peppers
2 (4-ounce) cans chopped black olives, drained

Dressing:
3/4 cup extra-virgin olive oil
1/4 cup wine vinegar
1/4 teaspoon dry mustard
1 teaspoon garlic salt
1/2 teaspoon fresh cracked ground pepper
2 teaspoons Tabasco™ sauce

Onion

Mix salad ingredients in large bowl. In small bowl, mix dressing ingredients and pour over pea mixture, tossing to mix. Cover and let stand in refrigerator 4 to 5 hours or overnight. Serve with tostado corn chips.

TEXAS TRASH™

This recipe is a variation of the old Wheat Chex™ Snack Mix recipe originated by the Ralston-Purina company more than fifty years ago. This recipe has always been popular in Texas and is standard in compilation cookbooks. A company in El Paso sells a snack mix called "Texas Trash"™ and has registered this name. This has not stopped community cookbooks from publishing the recipe under the name Texas Trash™. It also has been called "Nuts and Bolts," "Stuff," "Junk," and "TV Snack" just to name a few. This recipe knows no bounds. Once you start mixing it up, you will be pulling out crackers, cereals, pretzels, and anything else you can find in the pantry. The butter- and Worcestershire-flavored coating makes any cereal taste good. If you are making this recipe, my advice is to double the batch. The kids will gobble it up, and if there is any left over, it keeps well stored in an airtight jar or a plastic storage bag.

Jalapeño Café Snack Mix

3/4 cup butter (1-1/2 sticks)
6 tablespoons Worcestershire sauce
2 tablespoons Tabasco™ sauce
1/2 teaspoon garlic powder
1 teaspoon sage
6 to 8 cups of Wheat Chex™, Corn Chex™, Cheerios™,
    or any like cereal
2 cups tiny pretzel squares
2 cups tiny cheese crackers
2 cups peanuts
1 cup sunflower seeds

Pour melted butter into a large shallow baking pan. Add Worcestershire, Tabasco™, garlic powder, and sage, mixing well. Combine dry ingredients and add to mixture; toss to coat. Bake in 250° oven for 1 hour, stirring every 10 to 15 minutes. Spread on paper towels to cool.

SALADS, SAUCES, SOUPS, & MAIN DISHES

A Texas Staple:
RANCH-STYLE BEANS™

When we talk about the meals we ate as children, we tend to remember the simple everyday foods. I come from a large family, and one food we all loved was Ranch-Style Beans™. Everyone in Texas is familiar with the black can with white letters, and if you drive through Ft. Worth, you can still see the big sign on the old Ranch-Style Beans™ factory from the Interstate.

For those of you who never have eaten Ranch-Style Beans™, they are pinto beans cooked in a chili gravy. Many companies have tried, but none could ever match the rich Tex-Mex flavor of Ranch-Style Beans™. I don't think the beans are made in Ft. Worth anymore. The company was sold to one of the big food conglomerates, but you can still buy them at the supermarket for 55 cents a can. I served these beans to my kids and then to my grandchildren.

In fact, I sent a package of Texas foods to my homesick grandson, who is attending college in Rochester, New York. I put in a can of Ranch-Style Beans™. He later told me that he opened the can and ate all the beans without even warming them. I have been in supermarkets in the upscale areas of Dallas and have seen women, dressed in Chanel and Gucci, buying their Ranch-Style Beans™.

Nothing goes better with chicken-fried steak, cream gravy, and mashed potatoes than Ranch-Style Beans™. If you have never eaten Ranch-Style Beans™, give them a try.

FRITO™ PIES

I've always heard that this tasty concoction was created in San Antonio, Texas, by Daisy Dean Doolin, mother of Elmer Doolin, the inventor of Fritos™. According to Texas legend, Mrs. Doolin came up with the recipe in 1932 to help her son sell more of his new-fangled corn product. Twenty years later, in 1952, the Frito™ company got in on the action by hiring its first home economist, Nell Morris, who compiled a cookbook with recipes, including one for Frito™ Pie, to promote company products.

There is another story circulating: this one claims that Teresa Hernandez, an employee of Woolworth's in Santa Fe, New Mexico, created the first Frito™ Pie. In January 1960, sales were lagging at the store and the manager challenged his employees to come up with some new sales promotions. The Frito™ Pie was an instant hit and is still served at the Woolworth store's successor, The Five and Dime. For a while, San Antonio, Texas, and Santa Fe, New Mexico, were locked in a battle over who invented this treat. Santa Fe finally settled the controversy by claiming to have the best Frito™ Pie.

Wherever its origin, this recipe was quickly embraced by Texans and found its way to café menus, school cafeteria lunches, and high school athletic events throughout the state. It was the perfect mobile snack, a predecessor to fast food—easy to prepare, easy to eat, and you could carry it around in its handy little bag. Simply slit the Frito™ bag lengthwise on its side; add several tablespoons of good Texas chili; top with chopped onions, cheese, jalapeños, or anything else you like.

This recipe even moved into the family kitchen, and homemakers started serving Frito™ Pie Casserole, where the Fritos™ were spread in a baking dish, covered with chili and onions, topped with cheese, and baked in the oven.

I found a reference to "Frito™ Enchiladas," published in a 1946 Dallas, Texas, cookbook, *What's on the Menu. I can remember eating Frito™ Pie from the bag at a little café down on Elm Street in downtown Dallas in the late 1950s, long before *Cowboy Chow* printed similar serving instructions. Here is my recollection of the Frito™ Pie recipe from that little café and a modern interpretation of the 1946 recipe for Frito™ Enchiladas.

Frito™ Pie

One single-serving-sized bag of Fritos™
1/2 cup warm chili con carne
1 or 2 tablespoons chopped onion
1 or 2 tablespoons grated Cheddar cheese
Additional toppings: chopped avocado, ripe black olives, finely diced
    tomato, pickled jalapeño slices

Press on sealed bag to slightly crush Fritos™, then make lengthwise slit
along edge of bag. Spoon in chili; top with onion, cheese, and other
toppings. Eat from bag with plastic spoon.

Frito™ Enchilada Pie

3 cups small-size Fritos™ corn chips
1 (16-ounce) can chili with beans
1 small onion, finely chopped
1 cup grated Cheddar cheese
1 small (4-ounce) can sliced black olives

Spray a 9- x 9-inch glass baking dish with nonstick baking spray. Place
Fritos™ in dish; crush chips slightly with a large spoon or spatula. Spoon
chili over Fritos™ and sprinkle with chopped onion. Top with grated
cheese and spread black olives on top. Bake in 425° oven 15 minutes or
long enough to warm the chili and melt the cheese.

Olive Branch

BARBEQUED BEEF

Here is a recipe developed by Gail Moore, a transplanted Texan living in Rhode Island. Gail serves this "Taste of Texas" to New England friends, and it is always a hit. With this recipe, a homesick Texan can make some barbeque without spending long hours smoking meat over a charcoal fire.

Oven Barbeque Brisket

1 large (5- to 6-pound) beef brisket
3 teaspoons seasoning salt
1 teaspoon pepper
2 teaspoons garlic powder
3 tablespoons Worcestershire sauce
3 tablespoons liquid smoke
2 or 3 bay leaves

Preheat oven to 450°. Trim excess fat from meat and place in roasting pan. Rub seasoning salt, pepper, and garlic powder over meat. Shake Worcestershire sauce and liquid smoke all over meat. Add the bay leaves. Let cook uncovered 15 minutes. Cover meat and reduce oven temperature to 250°. Bake 5 to 6 hours or until tender, basting often. If meats are dry, add a little more Worcestershire sauce or liquid smoke. The last 30 minutes, remove cover and increase heat to 425° to crisp up outside of meat. Remove from oven and allow to stand 15 minutes. Slice and serve with pinto beans and Texas Potato Salad.

Good for leftovers, too. This meat makes great filling for enchiladas and tacos.

Bay Leaves

A BOWL OF RED

Nothing says "Texas" more than a bowl of steaming hot chili. The origins of this fiery stew are hotly debated by chili aficionados. Some say it originated on the cattle drives in South Texas, where the chuck-wagon cooks plucked wild chili peppers to add to their stews. Others say it originated in San Antonio, where the Chili Queens served the dish on plank tables in the open plazas for almost a hundred years. Another tale is that it originated in the county jails with the chilies used to disguise the taste of cheap, inferior cuts of meat. In 1977, the Texas Legislature designated chili as the official state dish. You can bet that at any given time somewhere in Texas, someone is eating a bowl of chili. It warms you in the winter and cools you in the summer. As long as you have some meat and chilies, you can produce this dish; the other ingredients are left up to your imagination.

Chili was a cheap dish to feed to the prisoners in the Texas jails of long ago. The jail keeper brought home a deer or some other game meat, and his wife cooked up the stew using the spices she had on hand.

Pioneer Jailhouse Chili

1/4 cup lard or shortening
3 pounds coarse ground meat (beef, pork, venison, possum, squirrel)
1 tablespoon cayenne pepper
2 tablespoons ground cumin
6 to 8 tablespoons chili powder
3 tablespoons sweet pepper (paprika)
8 cloves garlic, finely minced
2 tablespoons salt
1 tablespoon black pepper
1 quart water
3 tablespoons flour
3 tablespoons cornmeal

Heat lard in heavy skillet; add meat and cook until it turns gray. Add other ingredients, except flour and cornmeal, and cook 2 more minutes. Add 1 quart of water and bring to boil. Reduce heat and simmer 2-1/2 to 3 hours, adding more water if needed. Mix 3 tablespoons flour and 3 tablespoons cornmeal with enough water to make a thin paste. Add to chili, stirring constantly. Cook for another 15 to 20 minutes, stirring to keep from burning.

Classic Texas Chili

2 tablespoons oil
2-1/2 to 3 pounds beef (chuck or stew meat), cut into small pieces
4 to 5 tablespoons chili powder
1 tablespoon ground cayenne pepper
1 heaping tablespoon ground cumin
1 onion, chopped
1 teaspoon dried oregano (Mexican preferred)
4 cloves garlic, minced
1 (15-ounce) can tomato sauce
3 tablespoons masa harina or cornmeal

Heat oil in skillet and cook meat until it is gray. Place meat in heavy pan and add other ingredients except the masa meal. Pour in enough water to cover the meat to a depth of 2 inches. Bring the mixture to a boil, then reduce heat, cover, and simmer for 2-1/2 to 3 hours or until meat is tender. Add more water as needed. Make a thin paste with the masa meal and water. Add to chili, mixing well. Let simmer another 30 minutes; taste the chili and correct the seasoning. Letting the chili stand overnight in the refrigerator improves the flavor.

When ready to serve, warm up the chili, put on some Bob Wills Texas swing, get some cold long-necks and soda crackers, and invite your friends over to share your meal.

PINTO BEANS

Pinto beans are a staple in Texas cooking, and I wouldn't dream of having a barbeque without having pinto beans on the menu. When you cook beans, they should never go to waste as the leftovers can be made into *Frijoles Refritos* (refried beans) or delicious creamy Pinto Bean Soup.

Here is a recipe for flavorful beans, seasoned with jalapeños, tomatoes, and cilantro.

Charro Beans (Cowboy Beans)

1 (1-pound) bag pinto beans
1 small onion, chopped
4 slices bacon, cut into quarters, or chopped ham (optional)
4 ripe plum tomatoes or 2 medium-sized tomatoes, chopped
4 or 5 fresh jalapeño peppers, stems removed, coarsely chopped
4 cloves garlic, minced
1 boullion cube
1/3 cup chopped cilantro

Rinse beans under hot water for a few minutes to soften. Place beans in large pan, adding onion, bacon or ham, chopped tomato, jalapeño, and garlic. Cover with water and bring to a boil. Reduce heat and cover. Simmer on low 2-1/2 to 3 hours, adding water as needed. Cook until beans are soft. When beans are almost cooked, add boullion cube and the chopped cilantro. Let cook 10 or 15 minutes longer.

Served with warm flour tortillas and salsa, it's a meal in itself. Great with grilled steaks, too.

Pinto Bean Soup

A great way to use leftover pinto beans. Canned beans can be used, but are less flavorful than day-old home-cooked beans.

1 tablespoon oil
1 large onion, chopped
1 clove garlic, minced
3 cups cooked leftover beans with liquid
6 cups chicken stock
Salt to taste
Dash of Tabasco™ sauce

Garnishes:
Corn tortillas, cut into thin strips and fried crisp
Avocado, chopped
Monterey Jack cheese, cut into small chunks
Pico de Gallo
Lime slices

Heat oil in heavy skillet. Add onions and stir. Cook on medium heat until brown and caramelized (10 to 15 minutes). Add garlic and cook 1 minute more. Place beans and onion mixture in food processor and process until smooth and creamy.

Place bean mixture in soup pot and add chicken stock. Salt the soup and add a shake of hot sauce. If too thick, thin with bean liquid or stock until a cream-like consistency. Let soup simmer on low 15 minutes. Serve with garnishes. Leftover beans improve in flavor after a day or so in the refrigerator.

Frijoles Refritos (Refried Beans)

1/4 cup oil or bacon drippings
1 small onion, chopped
3 cloves garlic, minced
3 cups cooked leftover pinto beans, plus 1 cup of cooking liquid
Salt to taste
Grated Monterey Jack or Cheddar cheese (optional)

Heat oil in skillet. Add onion and garlic and fry until softened, about 3 minutes. Add the beans and mash with potato masher while stirring in a little bean liquid at a time. Continue mashing and stirring and add enough liquid to reach a smooth consistency. Season mixture with salt. You can sprinkle a little cheese on top.

Memorial Building, Fredericksburg, Texas

TEXAS SHRIMP

Shrimping is a major industry on the Texas coast. More than 80 percent of all seafood produced in Texas is shrimp. Shrimp and hot chilies go well together. Most Texas shrimp recipes call for some chili or hot seasoning.

Sweet and Spicy Shrimp

3/4 cup apple jelly
1/3 cup fresh lime juice
1 tablespoon Worcestershire sauce
1 fresh jalapeño pepper, minced fine
2 pounds large shrimp, shelled
    and deveined
Salt to taste

Prepare 12-inch wooden skewers by soaking in water for 45 minutes before using.

Combine jelly, lime juice, Worcestershire sauce, and jalapeño pepper in small saucepan. Cook over medium heat until the jelly dissolves. Remove from heat to cool.

Thread four shrimp on each wooden skewer so shrimp will lay flat. Brush both sides of shrimp with jelly mixture, coating well. Place on tray and allow to marinate for 15 minutes. Just before grilling, salt to taste. Grill shrimp 2 minutes on each side, brushing on more of the jelly mixture before turning. Serve hot on skewers with remaining sauce. Serves 6 to 8.

Note: You can substitute boneless chicken breast, cut into strips. Place one strip on each skewer. Increase cooking time on grill.

Texas Shrimp Gumbo

Texans love gumbo as much as the Louisiana Cajuns. There is a little difference in the recipe; Texans add okra to theirs.

2 cups fresh sliced okra or 1 package frozen okra
1/4 cup oil
1 medium-sized onion, chopped
3 cloves garlic, finely minced
1-1/2 teaspoons salt
1/2 teaspoon pepper
2 pounds raw shrimp, peeled and deveined
2 cans diced tomatoes
2 bay leaves
1 teaspoon Tabasco™ sauce
3 cups cooked rice

Sauté okra in oil about 10 minutes, stirring constantly. Add onion, garlic, salt, pepper, and shrimp. Cook 5 minutes. Add tomatoes and bay leaves; cover and simmer 15 minutes. Remove bay leaves and add Tabasco™ sauce. Let stand 5 or 10 minutes. Place 1/2 cup rice in bottom of six soup bowls; fill with gumbo.

Charlie Johnson Thrown from Wild Steer

CHICKEN

The Internet has many recipes for Cherokee chicken, with most calling for chicken, cranberry sauce, and bell pepper. Many of these sources say this recipe has its origins in a dish of quail cooked with wild berries. Here is a recipe that is easy to prepare and makes a tasty dish.

Cherokee chicken is not a true Native American dish, because it uses chicken, a domestic bird. But when different cultures meet as happened with the settling of America, one result is the exchange of foods and recipes. Hominy is an Indian food, which was adapted by early immigrants and became a food staple on southern tables. The American Indians also changed their eating habits as new food sources became available. A good example of an adapted Cherokee Indian food is Fry Bread, using wheat flour introduced by European settlers. The Cherokee cook mixed flour with baking powder, salt, and water to form a dough. The dough was kneaded and formed into balls and fried in hot oil. For special occasions, the Cherokees used to cook up quail or other game birds with dried berries. Here is a modernized version of this dish, using chicken and cranberries.

Cherokee Chicken

1/4 cup vegetable oil
3 tablespoons butter
2 pounds boneless chicken breast, cut into serving-sized pieces
1 green pepper, chopped
2 cloves garlic minced
1/3 cup chopped onion
1 can whole cranberry sauce
Salt and pepper to taste

Heat oil and butter in a heavy skillet. Add chicken pieces and cook until brown on all sides. Remove from skillet as browned. Pour off all but 2 tablespoons of the oil mixture. Add green pepper, garlic, and onion. Cook until soft. Add cranberry sauce, salt, and pepper, mixing well. Add chicken back to skillet; cover and simmer 30 minutes or until done.

Cerise Chicken

Here is another version of chicken cooked with fruit. This recipe comes from Georgia, part of the Cherokees' original homeland.

1 (2-pound) chicken, cut into serving pieces
Paprika and salt
6 tablespoons butter
1 tablespoon flour
1 teaspoon sugar
1/8 teaspoon ground allspice
1/8 teaspoon ground cinnamon
1/8 teaspoon dry mustard
1 teaspoon salt
2 cups canned, water-packed, pitted, red sour cherries
1 (small) can crushed pineapple
1 chicken bouillon cube
1 teaspoon red food coloring

Season chicken with paprika and salt. Sauté chicken in butter until brown. Remove chicken. Blend in flour, sugar, spices, and 1 teaspoon salt in butter remaining in the skillet. Drain cherries and pour the liquid into the skillet. Return chicken to skillet. Add pineapple, bouillon cube, and food coloring. Cover; simmer 30 minutes. Add cherries and cook 10 minutes more. To serve, arrange chicken on a bed of rice. Spoon some sauce over chicken and serve the remaining sauce separately.

King Ranch Chicken

This famous casserole was named for the King Ranch, the largest ranch in Texas. It covers three counties and more than 825,000 acres of Gulf coastal plains. The ranch has its own breed of cattle, Santa Gertrudis, and is dotted with oil wells. According to local legend, this recipe was created by the Mexican cooks on the ranch who had to prepare huge meals for the cowboys and oil-field workers. One thing is for sure: this recipe will feed a lot of people. In Texas, the recipe is made with Rotel™ tomatoes, a local brand of canned tomatoes with hot green chilies. If not available, use plain canned tomatoes and add green chilies, plus a few chopped jalapeños.

1 large chicken (3 to 4 pounds)
Herbs, onion, or celery, to season
1 large onion, chopped
1 chopped bell pepper
2 tablespoons oil
2 cloves garlic, finely minced
1 can cream of mushroom soup
1 can cream of chicken soup (optional)
2 teaspoons chili powder
Salt and pepper to taste
1 tablespoon Tabasco™ hot sauce
1 can Rotel™ brand tomatoes
2 to 3 finely diced pickled jalapeños
1 package (18 to 20) corn tortillas
2 cups grated longhorn Cheddar cheese

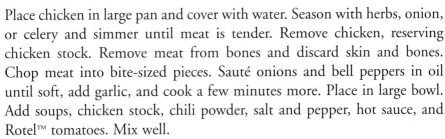

Place chicken in large pan and cover with water. Season with herbs, onion, or celery and simmer until meat is tender. Remove chicken, reserving chicken stock. Remove meat from bones and discard skin and bones. Chop meat into bite-sized pieces. Sauté onions and bell peppers in oil until soft, add garlic, and cook a few minutes more. Place in large bowl. Add soups, chicken stock, chili powder, salt and pepper, hot sauce, and Rotel™ tomatoes. Mix well.

(continued)

Heat stock and dip corn tortillas to soften. Cut or tear tortillas into large pieces and make a layer in bottom of a greased 3-quart casserole dish. Add a layer of half the chopped chicken; spoon on half the soup mixture. Make another tortilla layer, then another layer with the rest of the chicken, and layer with the remainder of the soup mixture. Another thin layer of softened tortillas can be added. Top with the grated cheese. Bake in 350° oven for 35 to 45 minutes. Serves 8 to 10 hungry people.

SUGAR FRYING

The recipe for Cherokee Chicken in the *Cowboy Chow* cookbook calls for adding sugar to hot oil when browning the chicken. This cooking method originated in Africa. African slaves, shipped to the New World to work on the sugar plantations, brought their foods and recipes with them, including the sugar-frying method. Sugar-fried Chicken is a popular Caribbean dish.

Sugar-fried Chicken

2 to 2-1/2 pounds boneless chicken breast
1/2 cup canola oil
2 tablespoons brown sugar

Make a marinade of:

1/2 cup catsup	1 tablespoon Season All™ or Old Bay
1/2 cup water	Seasoning™
1 small onion, diced	1 teaspoon pepper
3 cloves garlic, minced	1 teaspoon salt
1 tablespoon cumin	

Coat chicken in marinade and let stand 15 to 20 minutes. Heat the oil in a heavy skillet. Add brown sugar, stirring until melted. Add chicken and brown on both sides. Add the marinade plus 2 cups of water, bring to a boil, and simmer for 20 minutes or until chicken is cooked through. Serve with yellow rice. **Note:** To make yellow rice, add 1 teaspoon turmeric to water when cooking rice.

Sugar-browned Potatoes

The Danish also use sugar mixed with oil in frying. Here is an old family recipe from Dorothea Whitlock of Roundrock, Texas. Her great-grandmother, born in Copenhagen, Denmark, brought this recipe to Texas over one hundred years ago.

16 small new potatoes
4 tablespoons butter
4 tablespoons sugar
1 teaspoon salt

Cook potatoes in boiling salted water until tender. Allow to cool, then peel, leaving whole. Melt butter in pan or skillet; add sugar, stirring well until sugar is browned. Add the boiled potatoes and cook until browned on all sides. Shake pan frequently to prevent burning. Sprinkle with salt.

Dorothea says her grandmother served this dish with meatballs and red cabbage.

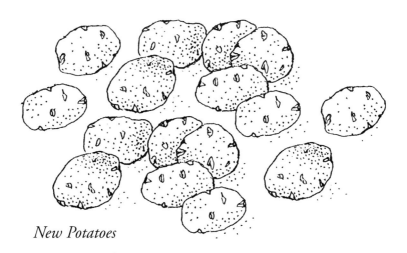

New Potatoes

CRANBERRIES

Cranberries have been a favorite of Texas cooks for many years. Recipes calling for these fruits are listed in community cookbooks going back to the 1920s. The baked version of cranberry relish seems to have been popular in the Houston area, as that is where it shows up most often in Texas community cookbooks.

I lived in Alaska for over a decade and picked many quarts of wild cranberries, which grow in abundance there. I cooked them up into every conceivable concoction: relish, jam, jelly, catsup, nut bread, cookies, sauce, and pie. The little red berries are high in vitamins, and with their bright color and pleasing tart taste, you can count on them to perk up an otherwise bland meal. I have never made a baked cranberry sauce, but I came upon a recipe using both fresh cranberries and dried cranberries (Craisins™). I am also including two more recipes, one for colorful cranberry punch, which is great for Christmas entertaining. The other recipe is for cranberry catsup, which goes well with venison.

Double Cranberry Relish

1 (16-ounce) bag cranberries
2 bags dried cranberries (Craisins™)
1 (14-ounce) can crushed pineapple with liquid
1/2 cup sugar
1/2 cup water
2 tablespoons cider vinegar
1/2 teaspoon salt

Mix all ingredients in saucepan and pour into shallow baking dish that has been sprayed with nonstick cooking spray. Bake in 300° oven 45 to 50 minutes, stirring every 15 minutes. This relish goes well with roasted chicken or turkey.

Cranberry Catsup

I used to make cranberry catsup from high bush cranberries when I lived in North Pole, Alaska. One of my neighbors had given me the recipe, which I misplaced somewhere along the way. Recently I found a recipe for the catsup in the book *Norwegian Touches* from Penfield Press. This sauce is great with game meats and poultry dishes.

1 pound cranberries	1 teaspoon cinnamon
1/2 cup mild vinegar	1/2 teaspoon cloves
2/3 cup water	1/2 teaspoon ginger
1 cup brown sugar	1/2 teaspoon salt
1/2 teaspoon paprika	1/2 teaspoon pepper
	2 tablespoons butter

Put cranberries, vinegar, and water in pan and boil until cranberries are soft, about 5 minutes. Put through food mill (or process in food processor). Add brown sugar and seasonings and simmer for 3 minutes. Add the butter. Serve at room temperature.

Note: Cranberry catsup can be refrigerated for months.

Cranberry Christmas Punch

1 quart cranberry juice cocktail
1 quart ginger ale
1 bottle Cold Duck™ (or other red sparkling wine)

Chill all ingredients. Pour into punch bowl and mix. Add an ice ring for a more festive presentation. For more "punch" in the punch, add a cup of vodka.

TEX-MEX ENCHILADAS AND TACOS

The Tex-Mex cuisine, so popular in Texas, is a blend of Northern Mexico and South Texas-style foods. The most typical recipe is enchiladas. Here are three enchilada recipes: classic Tex-Mex cheese, beef, and sour cream chicken. If you can't make up your mind, try them all, they are delicious. You can purchase canned enchilada sauce for these recipes, but if you would like to have the real Tex-Mex taste, try making your own chili sauce.

Texas Red Chili Sauce

6 dried red New Mexico-style chilies
6 ancho chilies
Boiling water to cover
3 cloves garlic
3 tablespoons shortening or oil
3 tablespoons flour
1 teaspoon Mexican oregano
2 teaspoons powdered cumin
2 tablespoons rice wine vinegar
2 teaspoons salt

Pull stems from chilies, split open, and remove seeds and white veins. Rinse chilies and place in glass bowl. Cover with boiling water; let stand 30 minutes. Remove chilies from water, reserving liquid. Place chilies in blender or food processor along with garlic cloves. Add 2 cups of the chili liquid. Purée until smooth. Add more liquid if mixture is too thick. Force mixture though strainer to remove bits of chili skin.

In heavy skillet, heat oil or shortening. Add flour, stirring to make a roux. Continue cooking until lightly browned. Add chili mixture, oregano, cumin, vinegar, and salt. Add enough chili liquid to make a thin sauce. Cook on medium low, stirring to keep from burning. Cook until mixture thickens and has the consistency of thin gravy. If too thick, add more chili liquid. This makes enough sauce for two batches of enchiladas.

Sour Cream Chicken Enchiladas

I have eaten so many bad sour cream enchiladas that I came up with my own recipe. If you don't like them hot, omit the jalapeños. If you do like them hot, use 2 tablespoons chopped jalapeños and substitute jalapeño Jack cheese for the cheese.

1 tablespoon salad oil
1/2 cup chopped onion
2 cloves garlic, minced
2 cups chopped, cooked chicken
1 tablespoon finely chopped pickled jalapeño (optional)
1 tablespoon juice from pickled jalapeño or
    1 tablespoon rice wine vinegar
1 (4-ounce) can chopped green chilies, divided
1/2 teaspoon salt

Sour Cream Sauce:
2 tablespoons butter
2 tablespoons flour
1-1/4 cups milk
1 cup sour cream
12 ounces Monterrey Jack or jalapeño
    Jack cheese, grated, divided

8 to 10 corn tortillas

Make chicken filling:
Heat oil in small skillet and add onion. Cook until limp; add minced garlic and cook 1 or 2 minutes more. Add chicken, chopped jalapeños, jalapeño pickle juice or vinegar, and 1/2 can chopped green chilies; cook until all liquid is absorbed, 3 to 5 minutes. Add 1/2 teaspoon salt or enough to correct the taste. Set mixture aside.

(continued)

Make sour cream sauce:
Melt butter in skillet; add flour and stir until smooth, taking care to keep from burning. Add milk and stir or whisk until sauce has thickened. Turn off heat before adding sour cream to prevent curdling. Add sour cream, grated cheese, and remaining 1/2 can green chilies, stirring to mix. Add salt to taste.

Prepare tortillas:
Soften corn tortillas by spraying each side of tortilla with nonstick baking spray. Stack tortillas and wrap in paper towels. Cook in microwave on high for 60 seconds. Tortillas should be soft and roll without breaking.

Assemble the enchiladas:
Spray rectangular baking dish with nonstick spray. Spoon enough sour cream sauce in dish to cover bottom.

To make the enchiladas, spoon 2 to 3 tablespoons of the chicken filling on each tortilla, add a little of the grated cheese, and roll up. Lay open side down in the baking dish on top of the sour cream sauce. Continue until all the tortillas are filled and placed in the dish. Pour remaining sour cream sauce over the enchiladas.

Sprinkle remaining Monterrey Jack cheese on top. Bake in 425° oven 12 to 15 minutes until the enchiladas are heated through.

*Jeronimo, world-famous Texas longhorn steer
raised near San Antonio, with horns measuring
9 feet 6 inches from tip to tip.*

Beef Enchiladas

Make enchiladas as described for Sour Cream Chicken Enchiladas, but substitute this filling for the cheese and onion mixture.

2 tablespoons cooking oil
1 small onion, chopped
1 clove garlic, chopped
2 cups chopped cooked beef
1 (4-ounce) can chopped green chilies
1/2 cup red chili sauce
Salt and pepper to taste

Heat 2 tablespoons oil in skillet. Add onions and cook until soft. Add garlic and cook a minute longer. Add beef and green chilies and cook, stirring to prevent sticking. Add red chili sauce and season to taste with salt and pepper.

Cheese Enchiladas

1 pound grated longhorn Cheddar cheese, divided
1 large onion, finely minced
12 corn tortillas
2 to 3 cups homemade red chili sauce or 2 cans enchilada sauce
1 (small) can sliced black olives (optional)

Mix half the grated cheese with the minced onion.

Prepare tortillas by spraying each side of the tortilla with nonstick cooking spray. Stack tortillas, place in paper towels, and cook on high in microwave about 60 seconds. The tortillas should be soft enough to be rolled without breaking.

Assemble the enchiladas:
Place about 1/2 cup red sauce in the bottom of large rectangular baking dish that has been sprayed with nonstick baking spray. Place one tortilla at end of dish; add 2 or 3 tablespoons of the cheese-onion mixture. Roll

tortilla up and place open side down in baking dish. Continue making enchiladas until dish is filled. Pour more of the red sauce over enchiladas. Sprinkle with remaining cheese. Sprinkle black olives on top. Bake in 425° oven 15 to 20 minutes until cheese is melted and sauce is bubbling.

To make restaurant style, place 2 or 3 tablespoons of chili sauce on dinner plate. Place two or three cheese-filled enchiladas on sauce. Spoon more sauce on enchiladas; top with grated cheese and black olives. If serving refried beans, spoon portion onto serving plate, too. Place plate in microwave and cook on high for 3 minutes or until cheese is melted.

Ham Tacos

This recipe is a new spin on an old favorite, the Tex-Mex taco. Instead of ground beef, it calls for a filling of cooked ham and potatoes. The tacos are fried to the chewy-crisp stage as preferred in classic Mexican cooking. The filling can also go into store-bought taco shells.

1 small onion, chopped
2 tablespoons vegetable oil
2 cloves garlic, finely minced
1 cup finely chopped ham
1 cup chopped cooked potato
2 teaspoons mild wine vinegar

Salt and pepper to taste
2 teaspoons Worcestershire sauce
8 to 10 corn tortillas
Nonstick spray
Salad oil for frying

Serve with:
Shredded iceberg lettuce
Finely chopped tomato
Ranch dressing

2 avocados
Mexican Red Hot™ sauce

Cook onion in 2 tablespoons oil until soft; add garlic and cook 1 minute. Add ham, potato, vinegar, salt, pepper, and Worcestershire sauce. If too dry, add 2 tablespoons water; stir and cook until mixture starts to brown. Remove from heat and prepare tortillas.

Prepare tortillas:

Lightly spray tortillas on each side with nonstick cooking spray. Wrap stacked tortillas in paper towels and microwave on high for 1 minute. The tortillas should be soft and able to be folded without breaking.

Assemble the taco:

Place a little of the ham mixture (about 2 to 3 tablespoons) in the center of each corn tortilla. Press filling together and fold tortilla in half. Continue until all tortillas are filled. Heat about 1 inch of oil in skillet. When hot, carefully lay folded tortilla in oil so filling will not fall out. Let cook on one side and turn and cook on the other. Fry until starting to crisp, but still a little chewy. Drain on paper towels.

Stuff with salad mixture, lay several avocado slices on top, and pass the hot sauce. *Bueno!*

Historic Texas Cookbook Advice
One danger of overeating—
it may cause you to live beyond your seams.
Don't put off until tomorrow
the things you should have done yesterday.

1913 Rules for Cooking
Have your hair neatly fastened back.
Wear no jewelry.
Wear a wash dress, if available.
Never dry dishes with a hand towel or apron.

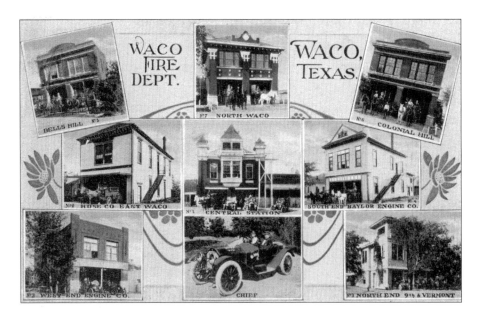

Historic Waco, Texas

In the Surf, Galveston, Texas

BREADS & PEPPERS

"exotic stuff or, like, corn bread?"

—Judge Samuel B. Kent
from the factual summary, in the United States District Court
for the Southern District of Texas, Galveston, Texas
Civil Action No. G-01-491

Corn Grows Big in Texas

Mama's Southern Corn Bread

1-1/2 cups cornmeal
3 tablespoons flour
1 teaspoon salt
1 teaspoon baking soda
2 cups buttermilk
1 egg, beaten
3 tablespoons bacon drippings

Mix dry ingredients, taking care that the baking soda is dispersed throughout. Add buttermilk and egg, mixing well. Heat bacon drippings in a 9- to 10-inch cast-iron skillet until very hot. Add batter and bake in 450° oven 20 to 25 minutes until browned on top.

Easy Monkey Bread

Great for breakfast, and so easy.

3/4 cup sugar or brown sugar
1 teaspoon cinnamon
3 cans ready-to-bake buttermilk biscuits
1 stick butter or margarine

Mix sugar with cinnamon in a shallow bowl. Cut biscuits into quarters and roll in the sugar-cinnamon mixture. Pile in a greased and floured angel food or Bundt pan. Melt the butter in a small saucepan and add the remaining cinnamon-sugar mixture, heating until sugar is no longer grainy. Pour over biscuits and bake in a 350° oven 30 to 40 minutes. Let stand about 10 minutes, then invert onto a large plate. For additional flavor, spread 1/2 cup chopped pecans and 1/2 cup raisins among the biscuit pieces.

Texas Muffin Bread

One level teaspoon soda—now
And three good eggs you'll choose—
A little salt, one quart of meal
And some buttermilk you'll use;
Then bake it quick and serve it hot,
And when your table's spread,
No kingly food you'll find so good
As "Texas Muffin Bread."

—from an 1895 Texas cookbook

Ranch Biscuits

This recipe shows up often in community cookbooks and is a direct descendant of the sourdough biscuits made by the chuck-wagon cook over a hundred years ago.

5 cups flour
1 teaspoon baking powder
1 teaspoon baking soda
3 tablespoons sugar
1 teaspoon salt
3/4 cup vegetable shortening
1 package dry yeast dissolved in 1/4 cup warm (not hot) water
2 cups buttermilk

Sift dry ingredients together. Cut in shortening. Mix yeast, water, and buttermilk; add mixture to dry ingredients. Knead dough for 2 or 3 minutes. Pinch off rolls and bake on greased pan at 350° for 35 minutes. Cover unused dough and place in refrigerator. Roll out and bake like rolls or biscuits as needed. Dough will keep for up to 2 weeks.

STUFFED JALAPEÑOS

Jalapeño peppers are the most popular chili pepper in Texas. They can be used in an endless variety of dishes, from stews to salsas. In my opinion, these little green bombs were born to be stuffed. Jalapeños take to cheese, bacon, peanut butter, shrimp, tuna, and just about anything else you can find. The popular name for a stuffed jalapeño is "Popper."

Here are two easy recipes for stuffed jalapeños, plus one for the ultimate Popper.

Tuna Jalapeño Poppers

This is a quick and easy recipe, sure to please.

1 can tuna, well drained
2 to 3 tablespoons finely chopped onion
2 to 3 tablespoons mayonnaise
Salt and pepper to taste
Chopped cilantro, small amount (optional)
10 to 12 whole canned jalapeños, split lengthwise,
    with seeds removed, drained on paper towels

Mix tuna, onion, mayonnaise, salt and pepper, and cilantro. Place a tablespoon of the tuna mixture on each half pepper. This recipe is great to make ahead, as it can be covered and refrigerated until ready to serve.

Crisp Stuffed Jalapeños

This is the ultimate Popper, more work to make, but by far the best tasting. Serve with a creamy avocado dipping sauce. Just try to eat only one! Great with frozen Margaritas or Mexican dark beer.

2 cups chopped, cooked chicken
1/4 cup salsa or picante sauce
12 medium-sized fresh jalapeño peppers
3 tablespoons finely chopped onion

Breading ingredients:
1 cup cracker meal
1 cup flour
2 eggs
1 cup milk
1/4 teaspoon salt
1/4 teaspoon pepper

In small bowl, mix chopped chicken with onions, salsa or picante sauce. It should moisten the chicken just enough for it to hold together.

With a sharp knife, make a slit along the side of each jalapeño, leaving the stems intact. Remove seeds if desired. Stuff peppers full of the chicken mixture.

Prepare breading mixture:
Mix cracker meal and flour together in a shallow bowl. Beat eggs, milk, salt, and pepper together in another bowl. Dip stuffed peppers in egg mixture, then in cracker meal. Repeat procedure. Set on waxed paper to dry for at least 10 minutes. Deep-fry until golden brown. Drain on absorbent paper towels.

Note: The breading will stick better if Poppers are placed in freezer for 1 hour before frying.

Bacon-Cheddar Poppers

1 (12-ounce) block Cheddar or Cheddar/Jack cheese
6 large fresh jalapeño peppers, seeded and sliced in half lengthwise
6 slices of bacon, cut in half

Preheat oven to 375°. Cut cheese into slices long enough to fit inside the pepper halves. Fill the pepper halves with slices of the cheese. Lay the half bacon slices lengthwise over the tops of the cheese. Place on greased baking sheet and bake about 20 to 25 minutes until pepper is cooked. Turn oven to broil to brown bacon tops, cooking for 2 or 3 minutes.

These Poppers are also great cooked on the barbeque grill. Just place on edge of grill away from hottest part of fire and let cook about 25 to 30 minutes.

RECIPE FOR A DAY

Blend unceasing prayer
with constant faith.
Sift together experience, knowledge
and initiative.
Strain out all malice, hatred,
intolerance and bigotry.
Mix ingredients with a good measure
of patience and humility.
Make molds one hour long.
Makes 24 hourly servings.

—from a historic Texas cookbook

SWEET STUFF

"bust out of the corral"

—Judge Samuel B. Kent
from the factual summary, in the United States District Court
for the Southern District of Texas, Galveston, Texas
Civil Action No. G-01-491

Cowboys

"Always saddle your own horse."

—Connie Douglas Reeves
1901–2003

Connie Douglas Reeves was the first woman to graduate from the University of Texas Law School and the oldest member of the National Cowgirl Hall of Fame.

TEXAS GRAPEFRUIT

Grapefruit cakes are a popular dessert in the Texas Rio Grande Valley and with good reason. This area is a leading producer of white and Ruby Red grapefruits. If you make this cake, canned grapefruit sections can be used if fresh grapefruit is not available.

Rio Grande Valley Grapefruit Cake

1-1/2 cups sifted cake flour
3/4 cup sugar
1-1/2 teaspoons baking powder
1/2 teaspoon salt
1/4 cup water
1/4 cup salad oil
3 eggs, separated
3 tablespoons grapefruit juice
1/2 teaspoon grated lemon rind
1/4 teaspoon cream of tartar

Sift flour, sugar, baking powder, and salt into a large bowl. Make a "hole" in the center of the flour mixture and add water, oil, egg yolks, grapefruit juice, and lemon rind. Mix well and then beat thoroughly until smooth. In clean glass bowl, beat egg whites and the cream of tartar until stiff but not dry. Fold batter mixture into beaten egg whites until blended; do not stir mixture. Pour into a greased 9-inch layer cake pan. Bake in moderate oven (350°) for 25 to 30 minutes until done; cake springs back when lightly touched on top with finger. Remove from oven and let cool 10 minutes. Run spatula around edge of pan and invert pan to place cake on rack to cool more.

When cool, cut through cake horizontally with a serrated knife to make two layers. Frost with the following Grapefruit Cream Cheese Icing and garnish with grapefruit sections.

Grapefruit Cream Cheese Icing

2 (3-ounce) packages cream cheese
1 teaspoon grated lemon rind
3 tablespoons lemon juice
3 cups powdered sugar
2 cups grapefruit sections or 1 can grapefruit sections
    (place grapefruit sections on paper towels to drain)
Yellow or red food coloring

Beat cream cheese until soft and fluffy; add lemon rind, juice, and powdered sugar. Crush sufficient grapefruit sections to make 1 tablespoon of juice or enough juice to make soft frosting. Blend thoroughly. Lightly tint icing with yellow or red food coloring, depending on whether the grapefruit sections are white or ruby.

To assemble cake:
Spread icing on bottom layer and top with grapefruit sections. Cover with second layer, then frost top and sides. Garnish with more grapefruit sections on top. (You can add a few maraschino cherries for more color.)

Historic Recipe for a Happy Day
Into each day put:
4 parts each of faith, patience, and courage
3 parts of work (if omitted, the flavor is spoiled)
4 parts each of hope and fidelity
5 parts of kindness,
picking off all specks of pettiness and littleness
1 part rest (if omitted, the flavor is impaired)
1 cup of friendly words, dash of humor
Pinch of folly
2 parts prayer and meditation
1 well-selected resolution
—from a historic Texas cookbook

PECANS

Texas leads the nation in pecan production, according to the U.S. Department of Agriculture. In a bumper crop year, the state can harvest 70 million pounds of nuts.

After the first frost in October or November, you will see Texans walking in the woods, vacant lots, and tree-lined parks, their heads down, stick in hand, stirring the fallen leaves looking for the nuts. Years ago when I lived in San Antonio, our backyard was planted in tall graceful pecan trees. When the nuts fell, I was visited by a hoard of two-legged and four-legged critters, come to get my pecans. The crows were most ingenious in getting at the meat inside the shell. They would pick up a nut with their beak and fly to the top of the garage and release it. The pecan would roll off the roof and land on the cement sidewalk below. The crow would then fly down, grab the now-cracked pecan, and take it up to a high limb to eat.

Pecan Pie (A Texas classic)

Early pecan pies called for using molasses or sorghum syrup. Then Karo™ brand corn syrup put a pecan pie recipe on the labels of its bottles. This quickly became the preferred recipe. In fact, 1920 cookbooks called the pie "Karo™ Pie." Here is this old favorite, easy to make and sure to please.

1 cup pecan halves
1 unbaked 9-inch pie shell
3 eggs
2 tablespoons melted butter
1 teaspoon vanilla
1-1/4 cups dark corn syrup
1 cup sugar
1 tablespoon flour

Arrange nuts in pie shell. Beat eggs; add melted butter, vanilla, corn syrup, sugar, and flour. Mix well and pour over pecans in pie shell. Bake in 350° oven 45 minutes. Serve with whipped cream topping or a little vanilla ice cream on the side.

Pecan Pie Squares

This cookie recipe makes a little bar that tastes like pecan pie.

2 cups brown sugar
3/4 cups butter
2 cups all-purpose flour

Mix these three ingredients and press into a 13x15-inch jellyroll pan. Bake 18 to 20 minutes in 350° oven. Remove from oven.

Combine:
3 slightly beaten eggs
1 cup dark Karo™ syrup
1 cup sugar
1-1/2 cups chopped pecans
1 tablespoon flour
1/2 teaspoon salt
1/2 teaspoon vanilla

Mix ingredients well. Spread over baked crust, return to oven, and bake 20 minutes longer. Cool and cut into squares. Makes 3 dozen.

Pastel de Tres Leches (Three Milks Cake)

This cake has been popular in Nicaragua, Guatemala, and Southern Mexico for many years. Some food experts say the recipe was originally printed on the label of canned milk sold in those regions. Latin-American immigrants brought the recipe to Texas, and Texans fell in love with its rich, creamy flavor. It is now popular dessert fare in Mexican restaurants from El Paso to Texarkana.

To enjoy the full flavor of this delicious cake, it is best served cold. Any remaining cake should be kept in the refrigerator.

For cake:
6 eggs, separated
2 cups sugar
2 teaspoons vanilla (Mexican is best)
2 cups flour
3 teaspoons baking powder
1/2 cup milk

For Three Milks sauce: (mix together)
1 cup evaporated milk
1 cup sweetened condensed milk
1 cup heavy cream or Mexican Crema

For topping:
2 egg whites
1-1/2 cups sugar
1/8 teaspoon salt
1/3 cup water
2 tablespoons white corn syrup
2 teaspoons vanilla

Make cake:
Beat egg whites until peaks form. Add sugar gradually, then add yolks and vanilla, beating for 3 minutes. Sift flour and baking powder together and add to egg mixture alternately with milk. Pour into a well-greased 9x13-

inch pan. Bake at 350° for 30 to 40 minutes until top springs back when touched. Remove from oven and cool about 10 minutes. Remove top crust from cake, leaving a ridge around the edge of the cake to hold the sauce. Punch holes in cake with toothpick. Pour the Three Milks sauce over the warm cake and place in refrigerator at least 2 hours or until cool.

To make topping:
Mix all topping ingredients in top of double boiler. Beat the mixture constantly while cooking over the hot water, about 7 to 10 minutes or until soft peaks form. Cover cake with frosting.

To serve:
Keep cake in refrigerator. Cut into slices to serve. Garnish with maraschino cherries or fresh, sliced strawberries.

Making Memories

I came across an old church cookbook and in this book was a dedication for each contributor who had passed away before the book was published. One dedication that I loved was for a woman who was "a maker of pleasant memories."

My mother, who died recently, was also a memory maker. What I remember most are the simple things she'd do, like baking a special dessert, cooking homemade soup, or sewing a dress for my doll.

My mother had a special cake she'd bake for different occasions: Christmas, Halloween, Birthdays, etc. On Valentine's Day, she'd bake a devil's food layer cake in heart-shaped pans. She would cover it with white icing and sprinkle crushed peppermint candy on top. What a treat for her six children; we always looked forward to that cake.

Today, children have so many more material things than we ever dreamed of, but when they are grown, I think they, too, will remember the simple things as being best of all.

—Carol Blakely

RED VELVET CAKE

Many people think the Red Velvet Cake has southern origins because it is so popular in the South. This cake actually originated in New York City at the Waldorf Astoria Hotel. This famous cake spawned an urban myth that began circulating sometime during the 1940s.

The story goes likes this: A woman was staying at the elegant Waldorf and after sampling the cake in the dining room, she requested the recipe. The next day when she went to check out of the hotel, $100 had been added to her bill for the cost of the recipe. The angry woman, with revenge in mind, started handing out the recipe, along with her story everywhere she went, asking that others pass the recipe and the story on. Sometime during the 1960s, this tale "morphed" into a cookie recipe from Neiman Marcus in Dallas, and the price rose to $250 that was charged to the irate customer's Visa card.

Whatever the recipe's origin, it makes a stunning cake. The white icing conceals the bright red insides until the spectacular moment when the first slice is removed from the cake. This cake with its red color is perfect for Christmas, Valentine's Day, and with a little adjustment for a crimson color, Texas A&M football parties.

When doing research on the recipes involved in the lawsuit, I found hundreds of Red Velvet Cake recipes, all with minor variations. Here is a recipe that I have used many times. I prefer the cream cheese frosting over the cooked icing that usually goes with the cake. You can vary the shade of red by adding less cake coloring. One bottle of red food coloring, which is the equivalent of 2 tablespoons, will make a bright pink cake. Two bottles, which is the equivalent of 4 tablespoons, gives the cake its popular deep red color.

The Famous Red Velvet Cake
(one of many versions)

1/2 cup Crisco™ shortening
1-1/2 cups sugar
1 teaspoon vanilla
2 eggs
3 tablespoons cocoa
2 (1-ounce) bottles red food coloring
2-1/2 cups sifted cake flour
1 cup buttermilk
1 teaspoon baking powder
1 tablespoon white vinegar
1 teaspoon salt

Cream shortening and sugar until light; add the vanilla and mix well. Add eggs, one at time, beating after each addition. Make a paste of the cocoa and the red food coloring. Add to the creamed mixture. Add flour and buttermilk alternately, mixing well after each addition. Mix the baking powder and vinegar in a small bowl and add to the batter. Blend well. Bake in two or three 9-inch baking pans that have been greased and lined with waxed paper or baking parchment. Bake 20 to 25 minutes at 350°. Remove pans from oven and let stand for 5 minutes, then turn cakes out on racks to cool.

The Frosting

2 (3-ounce) packages cream cheese, softened
1 teaspoon vanilla
6 tablespoons butter, softened
3 cups powdered sugar, sifted

Blend all ingredients until smooth. Spread between layers and on tops and sides of the cooled cake. If frosting is too stiff, thin with a little milk.

Seven Minute Icing

A prize-winning recipe of the 1939 New York World's Fair.

2 egg whites
2 tablespoons white Karo™ syrup
Dash of salt
1-1/2 cups sugar
1/2 cup water
1 teaspoon vanilla

Place all ingredients except vanilla in top of double boiler. Mix thoroughly. Cook over high heat, beating constantly until mixture forms peaks (7 minutes). Remove from heat, add vanilla, and beat until of spreading consistency.

Jalapeño Café's Margarita Ice Box Pie

After a heavy Mexican meal of enchiladas covered in a chili sauce, a creamy milk-based dessert is often served. This type of dessert is the perfect foil for the spicy main course.

One variation on the milk dessert is a Margarita Pie. Recipes for Margarita Pies first surfaced in the 1970s when liquor-flavored cakes and pies, such as Harvey Wallbanger Cake and Grasshopper Pie, were popular.

The first listing of the Margarita Pie recipe that I found was in a cookbook, *Texas on the Half Shell,* published in 1982.*

The creator of this recipe was going for the full flavor of the Margarita, because the recipe called for a pie crust made of crushed pretzels, which would add the salty taste you have when the rim of the Margarita glass has been dipped in salt. Most of the early recipes called for condensed milk and whipping cream, which resulted in a very sweet, rich filling.

* The recipe published in *Cowboy Chow* uses the ingredients in the 1982 book.

Here is an easy-to-make recipe that I developed using a prepared no-bake pie shell, whipped dessert topping, and frozen Margarita mix. Make this pie at least 4 to 5 hours before serving to give it time to set in the refrigerator until firm.

1 prepared graham cracker pie shell (large size)
1/2 cup water
2 packets plain gelatin
1 (10-ounce) can Bacardi™ Frozen Lime (Margarita) Mix
4 tablespoons sugar
3 drops green food coloring or enough to tint the filling
    pale-green like a frozen Margarita
1/4 cup tequila
1 tablespoon Triple Sec™ liquor
1 (12-ounce) carton whipped dessert topping
Grated peel of 1 lime

Place pie shell in freezer to chill at least 2 hours before making filling (a cold shell will make the pie set more quickly).

Place water in small bowl and heat to boiling in microwave, about 1-1/2 minutes. Add the plain gelatin to the water and stir until completely dissolved.

In large bowl, combine the Margarita mix, sugar, and food coloring; add the gelatin mixture and stir well. Place the mixture in the refrigerator about 30 to 45 minutes to chill. It should be just slightly thickened.

Add the tequila and Triple Sec™. Next, add the whipped topping to the Margarita mixture (reserve about 1 cup of topping to garnish pie). Use whisk or electric mixer to incorporate the Margarita mixture into the whipped topping. Beat about 2 minutes until thoroughly combined and uniform in color.

Pour mixture into the pie shell. Place pie in refrigerator to chill at least 2 to 3 hours. Pie will set firm. Before serving, spoon remaining topping onto center of pie and garnish with the grated lime peel.

SOPAPILLAS

This fried pastry is a popular dessert on Mexican restaurant menus. The pastries puff up like little pillows while frying, hence the name. A sopapilla topped with honey with a scoop of cinnamon ice cream on the side is a perfect ending to a hot chili dinner.

This recipe is a standard in Texas community cookbooks, usually listed in the section on Tex-Mex or Mexican cooking. I found this recipe in Texas cookbooks so many times that I stopped counting. It is so simple to make that recipe variations are rare and mostly deal with the measurements. Here is a recipe that will make a large enough batch to feed six to eight people.

Sopapillas

3 cups flour
2 teaspoons baking powder
1 teaspoon salt
2 tablespoons shortening
1 cup milk
Salad oil (for frying)

Sift flour, baking powder, and salt into bowl. Cut in shortening until mixture resembles coarse meal. Add enough milk to make a thick, stiff dough. Roll out to a 1/4 inch thickness and cut into 3-inch squares. Fry in hot oil until brown on one side; turn and brown on other side. Drain on paper towels.

Serve warm, dusted with powdered sugar or cinnamon-sugar mixture. Honey is usually served with this dessert.

TEXAS BUTTERMILK PIE

Texas cooks love buttermilk. They use it for biscuits, pancakes, layer cakes, candies, and pies. During the holidays when the cooks are operating at full capacity, the supermarkets sell out of buttermilk. I must admit that I use buttermilk for cooking every chance I get. I would not dream of making corn bread without using it, and my recipe for cinnamon buttermilk ice cream is always requested for family gatherings.

A traditional Texas dessert, Buttermilk Pie, is made from this tangy-flavored milk product. I think this pie started as a variation of that southern favorite, Chess Pie. Buttermilk was a by-product of butter making and most cooks always had plenty on hand. One day, a pioneer cook decided it would make a delicious pie. If you have never tasted this pie, you are in for a treat. My grandmother used to be famous for her buttermilk pie, and she always baked several for special occasions. Here is her recipe:

1-1/2 cups sugar
3 tablespoons flour
2 eggs, well beaten
1/2 cup butter, melted
1 cup buttermilk
1 teaspoon vanilla
1/2 teaspoon nutmeg
1 unbaked 9-inch pie shell

In large bowl, combine sugar and flour, mixing well. Stir in eggs. Add melted butter and buttermilk. Add vanilla and nutmeg, stirring to mix. Pour into pie shell and bake at 425° for 10 minutes. Reduce heat to 350° and bake 30 to 35 minutes more.

PRAISE TO THE COOK

Some men live that they may eat and drink
but wise men eat and drink that they may live.
We may live without poetry, music, and art,
We may live without conscience and live without heart;
We may live without friends, we may live without books,
But civilized man cannot live without cooks.
He may live without books—what is knowledge but grieving?
He may live without hope—what is hope but deceiving?
He may live without love—what is passion but pining?
But where is the man that can live without dining?

—from a historic Texas cookbook

Waxahachie, Texas

DRINKS

Looking North on Main Street, Taylor, Tex.

Taylor, Texas

Historic Ode to a Housewife

To love and honor are okay,
And one might promise to obey;
But what makes wives turn slowly grey,
Is what to cook each blessed day!

Elixir to Prevent Hair from Turning Grey

Melt four ounces pure pig lard
and add four drams oxide of bismuth
and four drams spermaceti.

This historic recipe does not say what to do with the mixture, whether to drink it or to rub it in your hair. I'd be willing to do both if it would work.
—Carol Blakely

MARGARITAS

The history of the Margarita is as fuzzy as you feel after sipping a couple of these delectable drinks. The Caliente Race Track in Tijuana, Mexico, as well as several bars in the same area, claimed to have invented the drink sometime during the 1930s.

According to singer Jimmy Buffet, who ought to know something about Margaritas, the most credible story is from the late Carlos "Danny" Herrera. He owned a restaurant called Rancho La Gloria at Rosarito Beach, a few miles south of Tijuana. One of his regular customers, a showgirl named Marjorie King, had an aversion to all booze except tequila, and she asked Danny to make her a better tasting tequila cocktail.

He experimented and came up with a concoction of three parts tequila, two parts Cointreau™, and one part fresh, squeezed lemon juice. He shook the ingredients together with some shaved ice and served the drink in a stemmed glass rimmed in lemon juice and salt. Marjorie loved it, and Danny named the drink "Margarita," Spanish for Marjorie. In the 1950s, thirsty college kids on spring break boosted the popularity of the drink, and it started showing up in bars on the West Coast. Then, some smart bartender placed the mixture in a blender and the frozen Margarita was born.

It took a Texas restaurateur to really put the drink on the map. In 1971, Mariano Martinez opened a restaurant, Mariano's, on Greenville Avenue in Dallas. He used his father's secret recipe to make frozen Margaritas. The restaurant and the drink were smashing successes—too successful. Because the bartenders could not keep up with the demand for the drink, they hurried, they cut corners, and customers complained that the drinks did not taste right.

Martinez knew he had a problem, and didn't know what to do. Then one morning he stopped for chewing gum at a 7-11™ store. There he observed a child ordering a "Slurpee,™" the half-frozen drink, and a light went off in his brain. What if he could convert a Slurpee™ machine to produce his most popular drink? He contacted top management at the 7-11™ headquarters, but they were not interested in talking to him. So, Martinez purchased a commercial soft ice cream maker. He tinkered with the machine and modified it to fit his needs. It was so large and bulky that he could not hide the machine behind the bar; instead, he placed it out in the open for all to see as it churned out a steady stream of frozen Margaritas. His invention contributed to the national popularity of Mexican food. The Tequila Makers Association, the city of Dallas, and the state of Texas honored Martinez for his contribution to the restaurant industry. Martinez did not think of patenting his machine; he was too busy with his new restaurant. He states, "At the time it didn't seem like such a big deal."

Unfortunately, Martinez's original restaurant recently closed, his space taken over by a national pet store chain. But thirsty patrons do not have to worry; Martinez has five other restaurants in the Dallas area still serving his famous drink.

Margaritas come in a variety of flavors, from traditional lime to pink watermelon. There are variations on a Daiquiri drink using frozen limeade concentrate, and it is easy to make. For a smooth frozen drink like a restaurant Margarita, our drink experts suggest freezing the fruits and juices into ice cubes before incorporating into the drink. Here are some favorite Margarita recipes as well as a drink for a thirsty judge.

Classic Margarita

In a cocktail shaker with cracked ice:
Juice of 1/2 lime
1/2 ounce Triple Sec™ or Cointreau™
1 ounce tequila
Shaved ice

Shake and strain into a chilled Margarita or champagne glass that has been edged in salt.

Note: To edge glass with salt, rub the rim of the glass with a piece of lime, then dip and turn the glass in a saucer of salt. Shake slightly to remove excess.

Tower Club Blue Margarita

The Tower Club in Dallas is famous for its many different Margaritas. This one is the most spectacular.

1-1/2 ounces tequila
3/4 ounce Triple Sec™ or Cointreau™
4 ounces sweet-and-sour mix
Dash simple syrup
Dash Rose's Lime Juice™
Dash Grand Marnier™
1/2 ounce Blue Curaçao™
Juice of half a fresh orange

Combine all ingredients in a cocktail shaker. Shake well and pour drink through a strainer into a chilled stemmed glass. Add ice and garnish with lime slice.

Easy Frozen Margaritas

1 (6-ounce) can frozen limeade concentrate
6 ounces of tequila
2 ounces Triple Sec™ (or Cointreau™)
6 ounces lemon-lime soda
5 cups crushed ice
Lime slices
Salt

Mix limeade concentrate, tequila, Triple Sec™, and lemon-lime soda in pitcher. Place crushed ice in blender; add limeade mixture. Blend until mixture is smooth and slushy. Pour into chilled glasses that have the rim salted by rubbing with a lime slice, then dipping in salt. Garnish drinks with lime slices.

Frozen Watermelon Margarita

3 cups watermelon juice
3/4 cup tequila
1/3 cup Triple Sec™
1/3 cup fresh lime juice
Lime wedges

Make ahead: Remove seeds and process watermelon for a yield of 3 cups. Pour the watermelon juice into ice trays and freeze until firm.

Make Margaritas: Transfer 2/3 of the frozen melon cubes to a blender; add liquor and lime juice. Blend until almost smooth. Add the remaining cubes and blend until smooth. Serves 4.

To serve: Pour into chilled glasses that have been prepared by rubbing edges with lime, then dipping in salt. Colored sugar can also be used for a sweeter and more colorful drink.

"Rootin' Tootin'" Wham

6 parts light rum
2 parts lime juice
1 part grenadine

Combine all ingredients in a cocktail shaker. Add crushed ice and shake well. Serves 4.

Historic Advice
*The smallest deed is better
than the grandest intention.*

Old-fashioned (Texas) Peach Slush

The Peach Fuzzy recipe is the blender-made version of an old southern favorite, Peach Slush. Peaches have a natural affinity for alcohol. The next time you make homemade peach ice cream, add a few tablespoons of good southern bourbon. The peaches and the whiskey marry up to produce a delightful taste. The Italians knew this little secret, too. A visit to Venice would not be complete without sampling a Bellini, the cocktail made of puréed peaches and Italian sparkling wine.

The hill country of central Texas produces some of the finest peaches in the United States, and it is only natural that the old recipe for Peach Slush would be modified to suit Texans' taste. I found the Peach Fuzzy drink listed in several Texas cookbooks published prior to 1988. It is also listed in many southern community cookbooks.

This recipe originated long before blenders and food processors. The secret to making drinks using peaches is to have very ripe fruit.

1/2 ripe peach, peeled
2 jiggers whiskey
1 heaping teaspoon sugar
Crushed ice

Mash together peach and sugar until sugar is dissolved; add whiskey and stir well. Fill large (12-ounce) glass with crushed ice. Pour peach mixture over the ice, stirring once or twice. Makes 1 drink.

Texas Bellini

Thanks to Judith Aldridge of Trophy Club, Texas, for this recipe for a frozen version of the Italian peach cocktail.

Fill a blender half-full with ice cubes and add:
2 large or 3 medium-sized peaches, peeled, seeds removed
(must be ripe peaches)
1/4 to 1/3 cup sugar
2 tablespoons lemon juice
3/4 cup Asti Spumante™

Blend until ingredients are puréed into a frozen mixture. Serve in chilled champagne glasses.

Hot Dr Pepper™ — A True Texas Drink

I remember a December evening, a few years back, spent at the Dallas Candlelight Christmas in Old City Park. The temperature was in the thirties with light snow in the air, and the entire park, with its old houses and buildings, was lit by soft candlelight. A choir sang Christmas carols at the church and Santa was talking to the children on the bandstand. A group of elderly ladies, probably from the historical society, sat at a table on the back porch of the 150-year-old Millermore Mansion, serving cups of hot Dr Pepper™ to the cold visitors. What a perfect Texas evening! Here is the recipe for this old Texas favorite, simple to make and easy to expand the portions.

Heat 12 ounces of Dr Pepper™ in a saucepan until hot
with bubbles rising to the top. Add two thin slices of lemon.
Pour into cups or mugs. Serves 2.

Gringo Gulch Grog

In America, grog has come to mean a hot rum drink, great for outdoor activities on cold winter days. The name originated with the British Navy, where, until 1970, part of a sailor's daily rations was a pint of "grog," a drink made of rum, water, lemon juice, and sugar.

To confuse the issue, Swedish settlers brought along their recipe for "glog" when they migrated to America.

This traditional holiday drink, more like a hot wine punch, began to be called grog in many areas of the country, including Texas. Different grog-glog recipes found their way into community cookbooks, with most Texas versions showing up in the Hill Country-area books, where the largest Scandinavian settlements were located.

Swedish Glog

A traditional holiday drink. It is also said to cure colds.

4 cups water
1-1/2 cups sugar
10 to 12 pods cardamom seeds
10 to 12 whole cloves
1 cup raisins
1/4 cup almonds
1 quart cheap red wine (burgundy or port)
2 cups vodka

Place all ingredients except wine and vodka in saucepan and bring to boil. Simmer about 15 minutes, then add the wine and the vodka. Bring back to boil and remove the pan from heat. Serve warm.

Grog

Here is a recipe for classic grog as served to the British "Limeys" of long ago.

Into a mug, pour a shot of dark rum.
Add a teaspoon of sugar, a little lemon juice, and a dash of cinnamon.
Fill the mug with boiling water and stir to mix.

Drink hearty, Mate!

Cerveza Roja — Red Beer

Cerveza Roja or Red Beer is an old, working man's cure for a hangover. It consists of a good lager mixed with chilled tomato juice. It has been called Tomato Beer, Red Eye, Red Dog, and Red Rooster. In America, this drink enjoyed a surge in popularity during the 1950s, and many brewing companies bottled it in quart bottles made of ruby red glass. The red glass beer bottles are avidly sought by collectors today.

Here is a recipe for a *Cerveza Roja* with a little heat.

1 (5.5-ounce) can tomato juice
Pinch of cayenne pepper
Dash of Tabasco™ sauce
Dash of seasoning salt
1 (12-ounce) can beer

Pour tomato juice into chilled 16-ounce beer mug. Add seasonings and mix. Pour in beer and stir slightly to mix.

EL VACQUERO COFFEE

The coffee plant originated in Africa in the Kaffar region of Ethiopia thousands of years ago. As far back as AD 1000, shepherds brewed a drink called *quhau* (that which prevents sleep). By the time Columbus set sail on his voyages to America, coffee was a popular brew in Europe. In 1723, a French sea captain took the first coffee plant to the New World, planting it on the Island of Martinique. Within a few decades, coffee plants grew in Brazil, Central America, and Mexico.

The Mexicans took this beverage and mixed it with their native spices and foods to create their own distinctive flavors. Kahlúa™, a coffee-flavored liquor, originated in Mexico during the 1950s, and within a decade was a popular drink in the United States.

New Mexico-style Coffee

The Chimayo Restaurant in Chimayo, New Mexico, popularized this after-dinner coffee made with Kahlúa™ and tequila. The drink first appeared on its menu in the 1960s.

1 cup fresh-brewed coffee
1 ounce Kahlúa™
1 ounce tequila
Whipped cream

Pour coffee into tall mug. Add Kahlúa™ and tequila, stirring slightly. Top with dollop of whipped cream and serve immediately.

Mexican Coffee

1 cup fresh-brewed coffee
Dash of cinnamon
1 ounce Kahlúa™
Whipped cream

Pour coffee into tall mug; add cinnamon and Kahlúa™ and mix slightly.
Top with a little whipped cream and serve immediately.

Iced Mexican Coffee

8 ounces fresh-brewed extra-strong coffee
2 tablespoons chocolate syrup
2 ounces Kahlúa™
2 tablespoons sugar
2 tablespoons cream or half-and-half

Mix ingredients and pour into two 16-ounce glasses filled with crushed
ice. Serve immediately.

Railway Bridges across the Rio Grande and the Great Customs Smelter
at El Paso, Texas. Mt. Franklin rising in the background whose
lofty peak reaches an altitude of nearly 8000 ft.
being the highest point in Texas.

El Paso, Texas

EXOTIC COFFEE CREATIONS

The flavor of coffee goes well with chocolate and is often used in desserts.

Easy Mexican Kahlúa™ Brownies

This recipe combines the flavor of coffee with ancient Mexican flavors: chocolate and cinnamon.

1 package brownie mix
1 teaspoon cinnamon
2 tablespoons Kahlúa™
2 tablespoons instant espresso

Icing:
2 cups powdered sugar
2 tablespoons butter
4 tablespoons cocoa
1 tablespoon instant espresso
2 tablespoons Kahlúa™
Milk, if needed to thin
1/2 cup toasted, sliced almonds

Pour brownie mix into bowl; add cinnamon. Use the 2 tablespoons of Kahlúa™ as part of liquid that is called for in package instructions. Stir the instant espresso into the liquid, then mix and bake brownies according to package instructions. Remove from oven.

Prepare icing: Mix powdered sugar, butter, cocoa, espresso powder, and Kahlúa™ together to make a creamy icing. If too thick, thin with a little milk, 1 teaspoon at a time, until of the right consistency.

When brownies cool, spread with icing and sprinkle toasted almonds on top. Let icing set; cut into squares to serve.

Coffee Angel Food Cake

1/2 cup sugar
1 cup sifted cake flour
12 egg whites
1/2 teaspoon salt
1-1/4 teaspoons cream of tartar
1 cup sifted sugar
1/2 teaspoon vanilla
1 tablespoon powdered instant coffee
Toasted, sliced almonds

Add 1/2 cup sugar to cake flour. Sift together four times. Set aside. Place egg whites in a clean glass bowl and add salt. Beat with mixer until foamy. Add cream of tartar and continue beating until soft peaks form. Gradually add sifted sugar, 1/4 cup at a time, beating after each addition. Fold in the vanilla and instant coffee. Stir in sugar-flour mixture, 1/4 at a time, folding in at about ten strokes for each addition. Pour into an ungreased tube cake pan. Bake at 350° for 35 to 40 minutes. Remove from oven and invert pan on cooling rack. When cool, remove from pan. Ice with French Coffee Icing and sprinkle with toasted, sliced almonds.

French Coffee Icing

1 cup butter, softened
1/8 teaspoon salt
2 tablespoons instant coffee
1/4 cup cream
1/4 teaspoon almond extract
1 teaspoon vanilla
3 cups confectioner's sugar

Beat butter, salt, and instant coffee until fluffy. Add cream, almond extract, vanilla, and confectioner's sugar. Beat until smooth.

DEFENSE FAVORITES

Pepper Hash

Ed Hirs, III, a Houston corporation financial analyst writes: "Here is one of my favorite recipes, Pepper Hash, from my grandmother Dorothy Davis Allen. Granny was born in Morrilton, Arkansas, and lived in Sherman, Texas with her guardian, and then her sister Grace Brice. Granny graduated from Southern Methodist University in 1927, and I took her back for her 50th Reunion."

12 sweet green bell peppers
12 sweet red bell peppers
6 to 8 hot peppers
12 medium-sized onions
1 tablespoon salt
1 quart cider vinegar
1 cup sugar
1 tablespoon celery seed
1 tablespoon white mustard seed
Sterilized jars and lids (prepared according to directions for sterilizing)

Wash, core, remove seeds from peppers, and chop into large chunks. Remove skins from onions, cut into chunks. Grind peppers and onions together. Add the salt and cover with boiling water. Let stand for 10 minutes, then drain well. (My Mom deletes the last step to preserve the vitamins.)

Mix together the vinegar, sugar, celery seed, and mustard seed; stir into pepper mixture. Bring to a boil and cook for 10 minutes. Ladle hot relish into the sterilized jars and seal. Allow to cool and seal securely before storing.

Note: This is great for hamburgers and other meat dishes.

Miniature Empanadas

Attorney Karen Tripp, Houston, contributed a number of recipes to our revised and expanded edition of *License to Cook Texas Style.*

3 cups flour
3 sticks butter
1 (6-ounce) package cream cheese
1 teaspoon vanilla
Pineapple preserves

Blend together the flour, butter, cream cheese, and vanilla to form a stiff dough. Roll out on lightly floured waxed paper. Cut into squares. Put 1 tablespoon of the preserves in the center of each square; fold and gently pierce with a fork. Place on a baking sheet and bake at 350° for 10 to 12 minutes or until golden brown. Serves 24.

The Beef in This Suit
"Stewing in Iowa" Roast

Dean Carrington, Iowa City attorney and Penfield's economic preservation consultant, says, "Here is the only item that makes me a hero in the kitchen."

2- to 3-pound eye-of-round roast
1-1/2 cups beef bouillon
1/3 cup cooking sherry
1/3 cup soy sauce
2 tablespoons browning and seasoning sauce
   (e.g., Kitchen Bouquet™)
1 tablespoon cinnamon

Place roast in a Crock Pot™. Pour/sprinkle the ingredients over roast in the order listed. Simmer on low setting for 10 to 12 hours. To serve, scrape off the typical fat membrane, then slice across the grain.

Optional: Strain the juice for gravy base.

High Country Hot Breakfast

Attorney Tom Riley's wife, Nan, writes that, "Tom invented this recipe one winter morning in Colorado before everyone went off to ski. It keeps well in the refrigerator, and every time it's reheated, it gets hotter and hotter. *"Spicy hot!"*

3 to 4 large potatoes
1 (10-ounce) can enchilada sauce
1 cup (more or less) grated Cheddar cheese
Olive oil to cover bottom of frying pan

Microwave the unpeeled potatoes for about 7 minutes. This is much faster than a conventional oven, and we don't have all morning. Dice potatoes, leaving skins on, and put in frying pan on medium heat. Turn with a spatula while they brown. When brown, add the can of enchilada sauce. Cook at low temperature for a few minutes. Sprinkle grated cheese on top and cover with a lid. Cook on low 'til cheese is melted. Serves 6 to 8 people. Nan adds, "How's that for simple?"

Potatoes for High Country Hot Breakfast

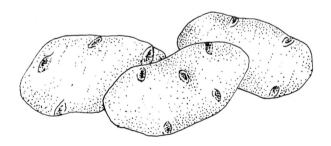

"Spicy Hot" Attorney Riley

This description of Attorney Riley's recipe might apply equally to his career. He served in the Iowa House of Representatives and the Iowa Senate in the 1960s–1978, where he had a distinguished career as a lawmaker. In his private law practice, he has represented clients in several high-profile cases against major corporations and successfully obtained verdicts in the millions. *Wall Street Journal* reporter Alecia Swasy devoted a chapter to his handling of the Rely™ tampon case in her book about Procter & Gamble titled *Soap Opera* (Times Books, 1993). Caroline Kennedy devoted a chapter in her book *The Right to Privacy* (Alfred A. Knopf, 1995), to his handling of the "motel peephole" case. Attorney Riley is the author of five books, three dealing with the law. He is included in the current and past editions of *The Best Lawyers in America*.

Chicken Tetrazzini

Attorney Bryan Aldridge, son-in-law and consultant to author Carol Blakely, says, "In the old days in Plainview (Texas), my mother made this dish with some success. It was one of her favorite fail-proof recipes."

2 to 3 whole chicken breasts
1 cup sour cream
2 cans cream of mushroom soup
1/2 teaspoon pepper
6 ounces spaghetti, broken into pieces and cooked
1 cup freshly grated Parmesan cheese

Poach chicken breasts in seasoned water, cooking for 25 to 30 minutes until done. Let cool, then remove meat from bones and chop into bite-size pieces. (Use spices you prefer in addition to salt to season the water.)

Mix sour cream, cream of mushroom soup, and pepper. Add cooked chicken and cooked spaghetti. Mix well.

Pour into a greased casserole and top with Parmesan cheese. Bake at 325° for 45 minutes.

Iowa Beef — Italian Style

John M. Bickel, Cedar Rapids attorney and first line of defense for Penfield Press, says, "This is great Italian beef! You have my permission to title it as you feel appropriate. It is actually my wife Med's Italian Beef." The Bickels frequently entertain large groups at their Mississippi River home in McGregor, Iowa.

4 pounds rolled rump roast
1 large onion, sliced
2 cups water
1/2 cup vinegar
1 tablespoon oregano
1 teaspoon garlic salt
1 tablespoon Worcestershire sauce
1 (8-ounce) bottle pepperoncini (in vinegar)

Place roast in a roaster pan; place sliced onions over roast. Combine water, vinegar, oregano, garlic salt, and Worcestershire sauce and pour over roast. Cover and bake at 275° for 3 hours.

Remove roast and allow to cool. Save liquid in the pan. Slice meat thinly. Return meat to roaster which has the reserved liquid, layering the pepperoncini (pour in the liquid from the pepperoncini bottle) with the meat. Cover and cook at 275° for 2 hours. Serve with Italian (or Texas) hard rolls.

Enjoy the best Iowa beef Italian style in the world!!!

Onion

RECIPE RESEARCH CONTINUES
TO SIMMER

Judge Samuel Kent ordered mediation. After the plaintiff's attorney responded to Attorney Karen Tripp that there was no point in mediation because we were too far apart, we faced other considerations. The expense of such a meeting would have cost Penfield Press $1,000 for the mediator and the same amount for the plaintiffs. Initially we offered $1,000 to cover Attorney John Timothy Byrd's expenses to the first meeting in Galveston to consider dropping the case.

Attorneys Hardy and Byrd were seeking "six figures" for deliberate infringement, plus attorney fees and court costs, which we estimated could be close to $500,000 or more. Attorney Tripp reported that only a large sum of money from Penfield Press would satisfy the plaintiffs.

After Penfield Press opened a website about the lawsuit, a lawyer in Tel Aviv reported a similar case decided in favor of the defendant.

In an interrogatory, Ms. Barbour claimed that Penfield Press was responsible for checking Jim Head's use of the recipes.

Following the advice of Larry Canter, a California attorney and son of Penfield Food Editor Miriam Canter, Penfield Press needed to find similar recipes published prior to 1988, the date *Cowboy Chow* was released.

Authors and friends across America joined the search following Carol Blakely's lead. **Esther Feske, compiler of *License to Cook New Mexico Style*, used the same definition of Pico de Gallo as "beak of the rooster" as in *License to Cook Texas Style*. She wrote, ". . . I send my blessings to you and all the wonderful people and not so wonderful people around you, your lawyer, the judge, the plaintiff and her attorney that ALL may learn and grow and find a way to make the world a more loving, safe, free and beautiful place to live. That's what I'm living for."**

As the trial date neared in August 2002, friends across the nation formed prayer chains and prayed individually for the publisher that this recipe lawsuit would be settled without undue economic loss for the publisher personally and for Penfield Press. They included residents of Iowa, Minnesota, Louisiana, New Mexico, California and other states.

Danger in Texas and New Discovery

"Underwriters consider Texas to be one of the most hostile environments as far as publishers/authors liability insurance is concerned. They always take a longer, harder, more zealous look at any application for insurance coming from any publisher or author in Texas."

—Mike Mansel, Certified Insurance Counselor
Counselor, Argo Insurance/www.publiability.com

Attorney Tripp discovered that Cookbook Resources, L.L.C., one of the plaintiffs, was using a trademarked name essentially like that of another company, Cookbook Resource of Milwaukee, Wisconsin.

Counterclaim and Settlement

Defense Trial Attorney Tom Riley, after reviewing Carol Blakely's recipe research, filed a counterclaim several weeks before the scheduled trial, stating that *"Cowboy Chow* was a compilation of long-established and popular cooking recipes. . . . Defendant Penfield commenced the painstaking effort to determine the merits of the Plaintiffs' claims set forth in their complaint. Investigation of this kind is challenging because thousands of cookbooks have been published, many in circulation which are available for purchase through retail sources but many more which are not because they are 'out of print' but may appear from time to time, if at all, in the market for secondhand books, which in the case of *Cowboy Chow* was first discovered by Defendant Penfield in an Oregon antiquarian bookstore in the Fall of 2001, after the complaint had been filed. . . .

"As the investigation and time progressed, more of the claimed copyrighted recipes were discovered to have an apparent ancestry in cookbooks published before *Cowboy Chow.* **However, Plaintiff Barbour contends in the lawsuit that she wrote the entire book, without disclosing that the recipes in the book were a mere compilation of recipes of others."**

Attorney Riley also mentioned the "failure of the Plaintiffs to seek a temporary injunction to enjoin Defendant Head from including the disputed recipes on his copyrighted website, other failures to take action consistent with a bona fide ownership right in the disputed recipes and with the ultimate goal of causing Defendant Penfield's financial ruin and the elimination of Penfield as a competitor."

After receiving Defense Attorney Riley's counterclaims, Attorneys Byrd and Hardy offered to settle for $10,000 and an apology instead of the thousands of dollars we expect they hoped to win in a jury trial.

Earlier, Jim Head told Carol Blakely that the plaintiff's attorneys offered to settle with him for $1,000 and an apology. Mr. Head, enduring treatment for cancer, was inactive in his defense.

Penfield Press agreed to pay the $10,000 request only because our defense alone had already cost nearly $50,000. Additional time and travel to Galveston would have further exhausted our meager resources. We gladly wrote an apology to Judy Barbour for our alleged infringement. We did not sign an agreement of silence about our experience with this recipe lawsuit—rare in the current history of copyright law.

Remember! The entire record of the lawsuit against Penfield Press is available in the Galveston Courthouse. Civil Action No. G-01-491.

We decided to share our experience in this copyright lawsuit as a service to others compiling cookbooks.

Cowgirl on the Alert, 1907

*Penfield Defense Attorneys Karen Tripp and Tom Riley
negotiated the final settlement only several weeks before
the selection of a jury in Galveston to try the lawsuit
in 2002. Riley is a nationally noted attorney. Tripp
lectured in Australia in 2004 about this case and
intellectual property rights.*

EPILOGUE

Discussions and essays about copyright rules continue. Issues relating to the Penfield Press lawsuit were overshadowed by the tragic loss of our grandson, Jordan Heusinkveld, 18, in an automobile accident in 2003. Jordan was instrumental in helping with recipe research on the Internet.

In 2004, a law professor wrote in a law journal about recipes, commenting on originality, social value, and copyright. He noted that the public has an appetite for copyright-free recipes. He additionally recognized the enormous problems in proving creativity and originality in recipes leading to copyright protection. Sometimes just a few words expressing an idea may be considered original enough for copyright in a poem. A word may be trademarked to offer more protection. Many ingredients listed in this book are trademarked to protect the food manufacturer. Titles are not copyrightable.

We discovered that what the experts advise about copyright in their books and publications and how attorneys and judges proceed may be thousands of dollars apart for plaintiffs and defendants.

There are very few recipe copyright cases and virtually no appeals to find in rulings in case law from past disputes. Shortly after the lawsuit by Cookbook Resources L.L.C., owned by Sheryn R. Jones, and Judy Barbour, author of *Cowboy Chow,* was settled by Penfield Press, a copyright suit by Coffee and Cale, authors of the *Four Ingredients Cookbook,* against Cookbook Resources L.L.C. was found in the records of the federal court in San Antonio. Jones had filed a countersuit. The outcome in this 2002 copyright case is unknown since by agreement all records were sealed.

Even if recipes are proven to be copyright-free in one court, this may not be the case in another federal district court as we discovered in our lawsuit.

Recipe measurements may differ in courtroom realities and problems may measure extra large in Texas.

THE SCALES OF JUSTICE

Judge Samuel B. Kent posed in 2005 in front of the Galveston Federal Courthouse for Penfield Publisher Joan Liffring-Zug Bourret.

In 2005, three years after settlement of the lawsuit, we visited Galveston to see the courtroom where the jury trial was scheduled in the lawsuit. Judge Samuel B. Kent graciously allowed Attorney Karen Tripp, Ruth Teleki and Joan Liffring-Zug Bourret to visit the room, where they discovered that he was instrumental in the historic preservation of the courtroom. Unique to this courtroom are the Scales of Justice Chandeliers, an original feature. This Federal Courthouse and Post Office was completed in 1934, under the authority of the Works Progress Administration.

"The courtroom was substantially renovated after commencement of Judge Kent's tenure in October 1990, including the addition of brass railing, renovation and repair of gallery benches and addition of cushions, new curtains and window treatments, replacement of substantial termite and water damage all along the south wall and portions of the west wall, repair of all chandeliers, addition of glass tops to counsel tables and replacement of all chairs inside the bar, recovering of jury box seating, repair and re-treatment of wall trim behind bench, obtaining of portraitures of all jurists sitting on the Galveston Division bench from World War II through the present date, addition of a smoke detection and fire suppression system consistent with historical preservation, replacement of the cork flooring and carpet, construction of a counsel podium, and substantial upgrade of the air conditioning system for the courtroom."

Texas Books by Mail
Prices subject to change

Stewing in Texas (this book) $24.90 postpaid

Mini books (Stocking Stuffers), spiral bound, 3-1/2 x 5-1/2 inches:

License to Cook Texas Style $6.95 / Postpaid $10.95
Revised and Expanded with recipes from Karen Tripp and Ruth Teleki of
Houston. This is the successor to *License to Cook Texas Style,* the edition
in the lawsuit.

Tales of Texas Tables by Carol Blakely $6.95 / Postpaid $10.95

Complete catalog of all titles $2.00

Distribution by:
Penfield Books
215 Brown Street
Iowa City, IA 52245
E-mail: penfield@penfieldbooks.com
Website: http://www.penfieldpress.com

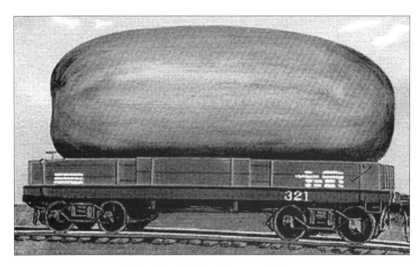

The Kind We Grow in Texas

*"My friends, the world is a scary place right now,
so hold those babies tight and give them an extra hug.
Pat the dog and rub the cat and keep on cooking.
God bless you all."*

— Carol Blakely

Cutting Out